KNOW Thyself

The Insightful Art of Palmistry

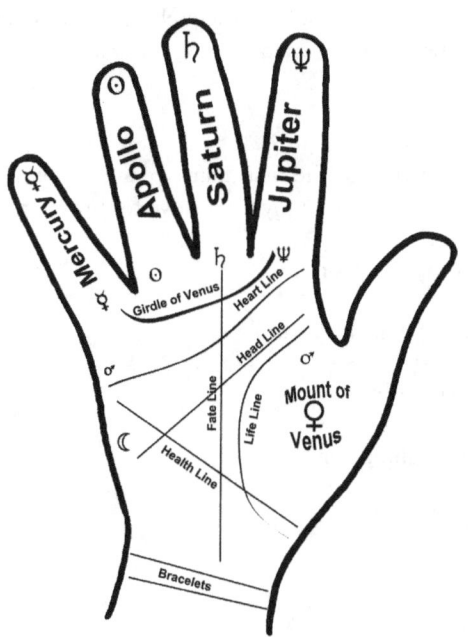

LUKE SHEEDY

Copyright © 2017 Luke Sheedy

All rights reserved. No part of this publication maybe reproduced, stored in a retrieval system, or transmitted in any form or by any means, electronic, mechanical, photocopying, recording or otherwise, without the prior written permission of the copyright owner.

The author of this book does not dispense medical advice or prescribe the use of any technique as a form of treatment for physical, emotional, or medical problems without the advice of a physician, either directly or indirectly. The intent of the author is only to offer information of a general nature to help the reader in their quest for inner transformation and spiritual well-being. In the event the reader uses any of the information from this book for themselves, which is your constitutional right, the author and the publisher assume no responsibility for these actions.

Acknowledgements

Thank you to Lorrie Lawler for the first draft typing and illustrations. A debt of gratitude goes to Chhaya Joynt from Joynt Creative for bringing this book to life.

This book is a work of non-fiction.

Cover / Internals Design: Chhaya Joynt

Inner Knowing Publishing ™

www.innerknowingpublishing.com

ISBN 978-0-9874968-5-0

www.lukesheedy.com

Dedication

To the two most important people in my life. My wife Julia and daughter Zara. The love and memories we share are the most important of all. Everything materialistic will disappear, but my love for you both will never pass. Appreciate and be grateful for each moment we spend together. Amass the wealth that won't desert you in death as a life spent on something that will outlast you is the ultimate lived life, so your lives won't be lived in vain. Remember this, the more inner riches you have, the less you need. Much love always, in this life and the next.

Peter Garozzo, who has been my lunch companion and confidant. Here's to glorious food and even better company.

Reid Heath, a man of such kindness and wisdom. Thanks for the cups of tea and the discussions about life on a wet and windy afternoon in your flat.

To my brother, David, it takes two men to make one brother. The bond that we share, will never be broken.

Know first who you are, and then adorn yourself accordingly – *EPICTETUS*

Contents

	Introduction	8
1.	History	10
2.	Intuition – with meditation	13
3.	Which hand do I read?	15
4.	The hand	17
5.	Fingers	35
6.	The thumb	56
7.	Major lines	66
8.	Minor lines	99
9.	Timing	113
10.	The mounts	115
11.	Bars, markings and signs	123
12.	Palm prints	139
13.	Strange influencers	143
14.	Rings	148
15.	Nails	152
16.	Guidelines to give a great reading	160
17.	A reminder	162
18.	Last words	163
19.	Further reading	164

God caused signs or seals on the hands
of all the sons of men, that the sons of men
might know their works. — *BOOK OF JOB*

To the Reader

I welcome you into my world. It's with the greatest of pleasure and happiness, that you come and take this epic journey with me into this fascinating and insightful art called Palmistry. By the time you have turned the very last page, you will have made many exciting and scary discoveries about who you really are. It's with the greatest of intentions and knowledge that this book will liberate you to be your true self. By adding more depth and insight into your consciousness that will open up for you, a new dimension to live your life to its fullest, this is my only wish.

Much love

Luke Edward Sheedy
Winter 2016

Introduction

*Lines have not been traced without cause in the hands of men.
They evidently emanate from the influence of heaven and from
human individuality.* — ARISTOTLE

Over the last twenty years, I have had the pleasure and the privilege to read palms all around the world for thousands of people. For the first time ever, I am going to share with you what I have learnt. The wisdom and expertise that I have amassed over the years, will now be put to good use in this book. For you to gain a greater insight and awareness into how great you truly are, with as much detail as possible.

The hands don't lie. There's no hiding with palmistry. The masks that you may wear will do you no good here. Let your ego take a long holiday, as I'm just about to present to you, your true character and identity, which is all out on display for all to see on the palms of your hands. To look at the hands is to look into someone's soul. Show me your hands, and I will tell you, who you are.

Our hands, and the lines on the palms are in direct communication with a large part of our brain cortex. More than any other part of our bodies, the lines of our hands are created by the nervous system and are in direct connection with our minds. It was the psychologist, Charlotte Wolf, who said, the palms of our hands are called, *the visible brain*.

Palmistry has come a long way since the gypsy fortune telling era of crossing palms with silver. The bigger the tip, the greater your fortune will be. Thousands of research papers have been published to bring this ancient art into the mainstream. Psychiatrists, psychologists, scientists and the medical profession have all been astounded and fascinated by the tested results. Which have been investigated at the Galton laboratory in London, and the University School of Medicine in Atlanta.

As I was writing this introduction, coincidently, I ran into an old work colleague, who I had not seen in twenty-two years, and he told me he was working as a psychologist at the local mental health ward at a private hospital. He went on to tell me that there are a number of psychiatrists that were using aspects of palmistry to identify deeper motivations into the human psyche, and discovering potential health risks was amazing. Due to this chance meeting, and being a mystic, I knew I was on the right path to write this book for you as I saw this as a sign.

It was Heraclitus that said, *"A man's character is his fate."* The large majority of people I have conducted palm analysis for, have been living the unlived life. They have gone on to be influenced by what other people think and say, conforming to the expectations of others out of fear of rejection, but in the process losing their own unique individuality and originality.

This is what the aim of this book will give you, instant insight. So you can identify and interpret the language of your hands. Enabling you to reveal talents and abilities, discovering the reasons why you have certain weaknesses and what you can do, to overcome them. By bringing this information out into the open, you'll bring meaning and purpose back into your life, with renewed vigour and awareness to where your true life will be lived and enjoyed.

Nothing will be left to chance, by studying your hands, you will be taking a positive approach and becoming responsible to understand your unique character. So you can develop and strengthen them. By becoming consciously aware, you can choose the appropriate mindset, and actions to live your life with inner fulfilment and contentment.

As in life, and so with the lines and markings of the hand, nothing is fixed, things are forever changing and moving forward. Life and time waits for no one. What you are about to learn and explore will enrich your life and give you a deeper understanding about yourself. Let me be your guiding light and all will be revealed as we interpret the maps of your hands.

As inscribed in the temple of Apollo at Delphi, *Know Thyself,* and pay no attention to the opinions of the multitude. Your destiny awaits you, it will now be uncovered on the palms of your hands.

ONE

History

Resolve to be thyself: and know that he who finds himself, loses his misery. — MATTHEW ARNOLD

The ancient art of Palmistry originated in India and China, more than 5,000 years ago. Many of the oldest writings can be traced back to ancient Sanskrit, Vedic and Semitic texts. In the laws of Manu (vi:50): *"Neither by explaining prodigies and omens, nor by still in astrology or palmistry, nor by given the advice and the exposition of the Mastras, let him ever to seek to obtain alms."* Even Prehistoric cave art of the hand has been found all around the world. Even before the written word had come into existence.

It was the great Greek philosopher, Aristotle, back in 350 BCE stated that *"Palmistry is a judgment made of the conditions, inclinations and fortunes of men and women from the various lines and characters which nature has imprinted in the hands."* In the Book of Job in the Old Testament, there is a reference to the significance of our hands, *"He sealeth up the hand of every man that all men whom he hath made may know it."* (37:7)

Cheiromancy is the interpreting the character from the lines and configurations of a person's hand. Better known as palmistry, it became most popular by the Greek civilisation. So much so, that they dedicated each finger to a Greek God. In this book I will be relating to each finger the appropriate God, out of respect to the early philosophers, who not only taught but practised this insightful study. One philosopher who comes to mind is Anaxagoras, who was well known for studying the hand as he gained a great reputation in his time to develop mastery level in this craft.

It was Hispanus, a Roman politician, who discovered a book on Cheiromancy on the altar of Hermes. This book was written in gold letters and it was given as a gift to Alexander the Great, the king of Macedonia. He was quoted as saying, *"A study worthy of the attention of an elevated and enquiring mind."* Lay people didn't study palmistry, it was only for the men of wisdom and knowledge to enjoy its wonders. These men included Emperor Augustus, Albertus Magnus (better known as Albert the Great, who was a universal thinker during the

Middle Ages), Hippocrates and Aristotle, who was also Alexander the Great's teacher.

Hippocrates of Kos, who was a Greek physician and is still known today as an outstanding figure in the history of medicine, used his knowledge of palmistry to aid in his work as a physician. Just like to this very day, many doctors, psychiatrists and psychologists still use aspects of palmistry to aid their diagnoses of patients, as my old work colleague in our chance meeting had spoken about.

It was when Europe fell into the Dark Ages, and the Catholic church came into power, palmistry was very much discouraged and the suppression of insightful knowledge was encouraged. It surely wasn't worth being burnt at the stake over, but many who practised palmistry, went underground, some quite literally. Heaven help any pagans or heathens practising such works of the devil. As this attitude persists today from my own experiences with closed minded and programmed people I have had the pleasure of meeting.

This became the time when palmistry became fortune telling and fell into the hands of gypsies and charlatans. *"Cross my hand with silver,"* the gypsy would whisper. Some making up creative stories about great fortunes and prosperity, or impending doom, depending on how much money was handed over to the charlatan running the show.

It was Marie Anne LeMormand of France, who brought palmistry back into popularity in the late 18th century. She read for many wealthy and influential people of her time, including Josephine, Napolean Bonaparte's wife. She told Josephine that her husband a general at the time, would be one day famous, for being a courageous and ruthless leader. Not only that, but she would be getting a divorce from her husband in the future. Bonaparte got so upset and angry with Marie's prediction, that he had her thrown in jail until his secret became the truth, and Marie was free to go. The truth shall not always set you free, but it did for her!

It wasn't until later that two Frenchmen tried to make palmistry more scientific and reputable. They both had palm readings in Spain which caught their curiosity, due to the outstanding accuracy of knowledge bestowed upon them. They both became fascinated and passionate about palm reading their whole lives.

The first Frenchman was Captain Carimar D'Arpentigny of

Napoleon's army, who became fascinated with all the different hand shapes called Cheirognomy. The second was Adolphe Desbarrolles who was a portrait painter and he enjoyed looking at the lines of the hand. Noting a person's character and destiny could be discovered there. Adolphe is considered to be the father of modern Chiromancy, to this very day for the great work and contribution he made to Palmistry.

This book would not be a very good one if I didn't mention another young man by the name of Cheiro. His real name was Count Louis Hamon, who travelled the world, gaining a reputation for reading for famous people and creating a massive fortune for himself while doing so. Cheiro wrote several books on the subject and some are still in print on his findings and what he discovered.

Last, but not least, William G. Benham, was the gentleman who elevated palmistry from fortune telling to a scientific analysis. He wrote a book called, *The Laws of Scientific Hand Reading*. And, today it is still used as the bible of palm reading for avid enthusiasts and professionals alike. His area of expertise was in health and what work you could do, by the study of your hands. The work he has produced and published still remains the most insightful and intriguing, even though they were published over a century ago. Benham devoted most of his life to his passion, authoring many books in the process, and influencing many generations of novices and professional palm readers alike.

This ancient art of Palmisty has come a long way from its origins in India and China more than 5,000 years ago. With the use of its knowledge in the medical and psychological professions, and the introduction in police departments using the study of the fingerprints, called dermatoglyphics, as a method of identification. The fingerprints are detailed, unique and difficult to alter over a person's life.

The most rewarding and influential achievement of palmistry is its ability to adapt to our changing society and still be able to offer insight and wisdom to those seeking the lessons it teaches.

TWO

Intuition

The thoughts that come often unwrought, and, as it where drop into the mind, are commonly the most valuable of any we have. — JOHN LOCKE

We all have been blessed with a wonderful gift of intuition, but unfortunately, the majority of people lose this inner sense by the age of seven. As we grow up, we are taught to pay more respect to rational thought and conscious decision. But the more contact you have with people, and the number of readings you do with people increases, so will this perception of inner knowing which will develop and guide you through your readings. When you have the knowledge and confidence to do so.

It will be the inner voice that the rational mind won't be able to decipher or comprehend. The gift of intuition is available to you at all times, it is innate in you. As you listen to this subtle voice, the more instinctive and non-rational you will become. This universal law applies to all things, the more you practise, the better your chances of improving and becoming more confident in using your natural abilities and talents.

Over the many years that I have been giving readings, the more intuitive I have become and it will be like you will receive images, impressions, clues, to what's going on in your friends and clients' lives, which tells a unique story about the person. The more your awareness develops and strengthens, the stronger the inner voice will be heard, and taken into consideration.

Visual tuning into your friends and clients, and observing the way they dress, express themselves and hold themselves in your presence is important. You need to be able to pick up on the clues that they give off, and this helps with interpreting their life experiences and circumstances. It is a significant quality for you to have as you can conduct the reading in the most favourable of ways. This helps produce a positive and informative outlining of information in a way that suits their particular character and level of understanding.

For you to be able to develop your intuition, you need to let go and trust this natural ability. Solitude and silence are some of the key ingredients to listening to the voice within. Meditating is a great way to quieten the mind, and get rid of all the noise and raciness. The benefits will be outstanding, not only when you are doing your palmistry, but you will be calmer and won't react to the challenges or obstacles that would normally get you bent out of shape and irritated, especially in today's fast paced society.

A simple meditation

Always go to a nice quiet environment where you feel most comfortable. Turn off your phone, there must be no distractions. Please devote 10-15 minutes of your time to this worthwhile activity. The benefits will work instantly and change your life forever when exercised daily.

Sit upright in a comfortable chair with your back up against the back support, with your feet shoulder width apart. Shut your eyes and put the tip of your tongue onto the roof of your mouth. Now, I want you to visualise a golden light around your body to cleanse your aura. Picture a golden shaft of light going through the top part of your head and cleansing the inside of your body of any ill health, aches or pains. Now, visualise the soles of your feet growing roots like a tree to ground you to Mother Earth for stability. Through your nostrils, breathe in nice and deeply, into the pit of your stomach, feeling your chest rise and expand. And on the out breath, release all tension and stress out of your body, feeling lighter and stress free. Let your thoughts come and go like waves on an ocean, but pay no attention to them, and they will subside. Draw your focus back to your breathing.

Continue practising this meditation and gradually increase the time, when you feel more comfortable. To get the most benefit, practise each day for the best results.

> The only tyrant I accept in this world, is the still small voice within. — MAHATMA GANDHI

THREE

Which hand do I read?

He who knows others is wise; he who knows himself is enlightened. — *LAO TZU*

The majority of palm readers grab the right hand first. But this can be a mistake. You must first ask your client what is the hand they use the most throughout the day. This is called the Active or Dominant hand. The other hand is called the Passive hand. So if you're a right handed person, this will be your dominant hand, and the left is your passive hand, and vice versa for a left handed person.

If your friend or client doesn't know what hand is the most active, sometimes found in ambidextrous people, ask them what is the hand that they write with, and consider this the active hand. To make sure that the correct hand has been chosen, compare the stiffness of the thumbs. Pull each thumb back gently towards the wrist, the stiffest is considered the active hand.

Left hand

"Length of days is in her right hand, riches and honour are in her left." (Proverbs 3:16). Traditionally, the left hand shows our potential and what we have inherited from our ancestors. It is the yin aspect of our personality, the reflective, intuitive and the inner person. This is the true self, without any masks being worn to make up for our insecurities. The side that no one gets to see, the shadow self. The past is found here before the age of twenty-one, this includes early childhood, teenage and early adult. What you have learnt and maybe what you would like to forget.

The dominant/active hand

This is the conscious part of us. How we interact with everyone and what we put on display for others to see. It's the yang, masculine energy and what we're doing with the talents and abilities we have been blessed with. The outer dimension of who we tend to portray to others is seen here. As you will find out, the majority of people have a lot of differences between the passive and the active hands.

If you're reading for a friend or client who is twenty-one or under, begin with the passive hand as it will give you a great amount of detail about their talents, abilities, limitations and how they are living their lives up until now. Then you can go to the active hand, which is what they will make of themselves by what they have been given. Always compare the two hands. The passive hand can be seen as the past, and the future found on the active hand, and what they have made of themselves with their particular characteristics and abilities which are unique to this person only and no one else.

A great, reputable palmist will always read both hands and compare their findings. If both hands are identical, the person is using all of their skills, and are well balanced between the inner and outer worlds. The more a friend, loved one or client is working on themselves, through study, workshops, reading books and putting more of an emphasis on self-actualisation, the greater the difference will be found between the passive and dominant hand.

A lot of people give up or give in to the pressures of society and its restraints unfortunately, due to job security, a need to make a living, the responsibility of children and paying a mortgage. So the potentials and talents lay dormant and repressed. Until one day, time and life circumstances may change and these unique gifts and characters of the higher self are channelled providing a deeper meaning and inner contentment which may never have been used, without action and effort on their behalf.

The lines in our hands do change over time, depending on the challenges and circumstances that only life can bring us. But the lines will change in a much more positive way, when we take the initiative to use our imagination and create opportunities to live a much happier and fruitful way. May the story of your hands provide and tell an inspirational and fascinating one.

FOUR

The Hand

*Often the hands will solve a mystery that the
intellect has struggled with in vain.* — CARL JUNG

IT'S IN THE TOUCH

All over the palm of the hand are skin ridges, and they contain nerve sensors. Their job is to relate how hot or cold the temperature of the environment is. By placing your hand on a hot plate, the nerve sensors signal back to the brain to alert of pain or discomfort (never do this.)

The finer the skin, the more nerve endings are present. The texture of the skin refers to how sensitive the friend or client is to their environment, and how well they react or respond naturally to those around them.

People who have hard, thick, coarse skin, don't pick up on many signals from people and their environment. They are not as receptive as a fine skinned person. Coarse skinned people can cut themselves and not even know about it and go about their business. They can walk into a room where an argument has just taken place and not pick up on the tension around them. Ask a person with delicate skin about the cut they have on their hands, and they will surely tell you how much blood they lost, how they endured and at what time the incident took place. As soon as a fine skinned person walks into a room, after an argument has just happened, they will feel it and most probably walk out. The finer the skin, the more sensitive and receptive a person is.

WHAT SKIN TYPE ARE YOU?

The quickest and easiest way to determine the quality of someone's skin type, is to run your index (Jupiter) finger length ways across the palm. There are four skin types, and they are:

1. Silk skin — artistic, creative, emotional, secretive.

When the skin feels silky smooth and soft to touch, this is the finest quality. These people are called Sensitives, both men and women have this quality, but more so on women's hands. Always intuitive with people and their environment, they can pick up on the most subtle of observations. Like the fluff on your jacket or dust on the top of your television. Often, psychic and always on time, they stay away from noisy environments and loud people. If they linger too long, their energy will be drained. Their house is always immaculate, with nothing ever out of place. Usually on the thin and pale side and are known to have skin problems, stomach disorders and allergies. Vitality and strength are not their strong points, due to a weak and frail constitution.

These people are rescuers and will be found in the health and healing professions. Most commonly, they are counsellors, healers, marriage therapists, social workers, teachers, psychics and in the clergy.

Drugs or alcohol affect these people immediately, and they can become intoxicated by drinking a couple of glasses of wine. These people are too eager to please others, especially others who won't reciprocate, or appreciate what they do. They need to love themselves more, and enjoy life now as they can be too serious at times. The hand which has silky skin most of the time has a long palm, with long fingers, and is known as **the Water hand**.

2. Paper skin — intellectual, curious mind, a love of study and communication.

Quite common for over half of the people I have read for. Dry to the touch, their hands belong to the communicators of this world. Visually and verbally, they like their technological gadgets and use them as a conduit to express themselves. Often found in public relations, media, television, secretarial, journalism, writers and marketing. Ideas, words and images mean a lot and they usually have a short square palm, long fingers with pronounced knuckles, long little (Mercury) finger, and a small Mount of Venus, which makes them enjoy the indoors more than the outdoors. The hand which has paper skin most of the time is known as **the Air hand**. People who have pronounced knuckles, like to bounce ideas and insights around in their minds before making decisions. Anyone who has a long little (Mercury) finger, are often found on these air hands, enjoys the love of words and have a great vocabulary, and also has good communication skills, both written and verbally.

3. Grainy skin — adventurous, risk takers, energetic.

As we are going through the skin types, the skin texture is getting slightly rougher, and the lines are getting clearer to see. These people are the doers who like action, and enjoy outdoor activities in which they excel. This skin type is found on men most of the time, but they're not as sensitive as men with silky skin. Boredom is not on their bucket list, and they need to get stuck into life. They play it cool when it comes to displaying any type of affection, and prefer to go to the gym, hiking, camping and release their pent up energy in these pursuits. Pressure and excitement is what they thrive on, and enjoy taking risks. They are often found in the police service, fire fighters, and stock brokers. They are passionate and adventurous, which gives them the thrill to keep themselves happy in life. The hand which has grainy skin most of the time, has a long palm, short fingers and is known as **the Fire hand**.

4. Coarse skin — practical, conventional, productive, not emotional.

As the name suggests, this skin type is just like sand paper to touch, dry, thick and hard. The skin ridges can be seen readily, and there are not too many minor lines visible. Men are the majority with this skin type, and they love the great outdoors and hate to be locked up on a rainy day. Most of them work with their hands and keep the country moving forward. Farmers, all types of trade workers, builders, carpenters, gardeners, mechanics, truck drivers and brick layers have this type of skin.

There are always cuts and scratches on their hands. There is never too much feeling in their hands and they won't have noticed where or when they have cut themselves. The fingers are usually short with a thick palm, accompanied by a large Mount of Venus. Showing a huge amount of zest, passion and vitality, people with coarse skin don't like formal situations and can be quite cold and non-attached when it comes to showing displays of affection and emotions. The temperature never seems to bother them as they can be seen wearing a singlet on a cold, rainy day. If you can get them to talk about their feelings, you are considered very close, and they trust you a great deal. The hand which has coarse skin most of the time, has a short palm, with short fingers and is known as **the Earth hand**.

WHAT'S YOUR COLOUR?

The colour of our hands represent life and vitality.

Pink coloured hands: are considered the normal, basic colour, with a good amount of health, vitality and blood circulation.

Red hands: A great amount of high energy and enthusiasm for life. At times, these people have a high opinion of themselves and can be quite overwhelming, and some people may find them a little too much to take. They are prone to outbursts of anger if they don't get their own way.

Yellow hands: These people can be quite pessimistic, depressive, or have a cynical type of nature. At times, there can be signs of no energy or vitality due to an excess of bile throughout the body. There can be an imbalance with the Gall Bladder.

Blue hands: These occur when there is poor circulation throughout the body. Chest infections and respiratory conditions like bronchitis, asthma and pneumonia are quite common. Energy and vitality can be quite low. These people often have the flu, around winter time.

White hands: In general, people who have white hands have low immunity, and have a weak disposition. They enjoy their own company and most of the time have lost interest in the society in which they live.

Pale hands: Most of the time, lack of vitality and vigour to live a normal life, can be a concern. Usually shy and prefer to be locked away from the trials and tribulations of other people. They enjoy their own company. The spiritual aspects of life interest these people. Walks through nature revitalises them and makes them refreshed.

ARE THE HANDS MOIST OR DRY?

Moist

Moist handed people are quite nervous, sensitive, anxious and concerned about what may or may not happen. They can denote self-interest and sensuality. Lovers of luxury, they have been known to over indulge at times, and are prone to being overweight and having dependences. Following one's intuition and how they feel is a positive trait of the moist handed person.

Dry

Dry handed people enjoy the great outdoors and have plenty of vitality for enjoying life. They over-rationalise at times, which makes them prone to headaches, neck and should tension. They have books around the house and they like to learn new information. They can suffer from stomach complaints and they tend to avoid spicy food. They need to drink a lot of water during the day, and they can become dehydrated quite easily.

FEELING THE HAND

Smooth and soft

These people like to dream and enjoy using their imagination. They're creative and at times can be quite spontaneous. They love beautiful surroundings and are sensitive to music and the arts. At times, they can be quite vain and only have their interests at heart. Romance and falling in love is very special to these people. With good food and elegant tastes they like to indulge in the finer things of life.

Very bony with knotty joints

Lovers of knowlege, they always have a book in their hands or close by. They love to debate and bounce ideas around until they've made up their minds. Thought and reflection consumes their day when they're not reading a book or article. Not one for giving in and standing their ground, they can be quite stubborn. Worrying is a hobby and when not in the mood, they can be tactless and rude.

Hard and thin

These people love their own company, and don't like change. As a consequence, they don't have too many friends, and are always suffering from the flu or something worse. They don't like to give too much of themselves and can be seen as quite pessimistic.

FLEXIBILITY OF THE FINGERS

Flexible

When the fingers are easy to pull back towards the wrist, these people like to go along with the crowd. They're adaptable when put into a new situation, they enjoy life and the challenges that it brings.

Socialising and having many interests keeps life exciting and fresh.

Stiff

Just like their owners, their fingers can be quite unwilling to give an inch, and are quite determined not to budge on anything. Change is always a disaster for them, as they have fixed attitudes and beliefs. The stiffer the fingers, the stiffer the demeanour.

DIVISIONS OF ENERGY WITHIN THE HAND

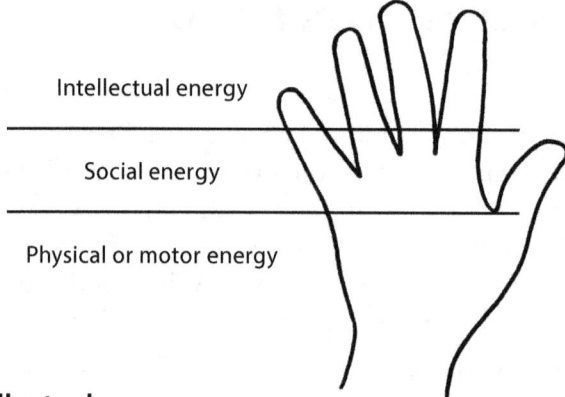

Intellectual

People's hopes and wishes which are within their very mindsets, can be found when looking at the fingers. The fingers constitute how a person thinks and how they see life and its challenges. Spiritual matters are a priority for this type of person, and are when the fingers are the strongest part of the hand. Questions such as, Are they living the life they want? What's the meaning of all life? What religion best suits them? These are but a few of the questions being asked when the fingers are long. Not only that, they also go into every detail. Short fingered people are often quick to find solutions to problems and can be seen as quite impulsive.

Social

From the base of the fingers to the top of where the thumb leaves the hand, represents the social aspect of our lives. If it's full and thick, these people have many friends and like to socialise with many different people. If this area is thin, and flat, the person usually has one or two friends, as well as preferring their own company. Most of the time they will enjoy a night in.

Physical

From the wrist to where the thumb leaves the hand, this is the physical and material aspect of our lives. This is driven by basic instincts, desires and the need for financial and emotional security. If the bottom half is thick and full, they have a lot of vitality and energy for life. Whether it is out playing various sports, climbing a mountain or going to the gym, whatever gives them a thrill to be active. These people can be quite touchy to get the full apprehension of the person or object. Listening and thinking is not enough, these people like to feel. If this area is flat, there is not much vitality or enthusiasm for life. These people can be seen as quite cold and distant, sometimes not wanting to take any risks at all. They prefer and seek their own company.

THE SIZE OF THE HAND COMPARED TO THE PERSON

Large

Large handed people like to go into detail about everything they do. They like to know the nuts and bolts about every finer detail, before starting a new project.

I once read for a lady who had large hands. She was complaining about the taxi driver who had driven her to the reading. She outlined how he took her down the wrong street, his car was a mess, and he hadn't combed his hair. I asked her if she ever considered becoming a dentist, because people with large hands enjoy fine, delicate work. She told me that she had thought about it the day before. Often you will find people with large hands working with jewellery, servicing watches, as dentists, or the arts and crafts. Remember the devil is in the detail with large handed people.

Average

People with average sized hands like to think about the situation before making a decision. They don't get too flustered about too much detail or get taken away with the bigger picture with what they're doing. The majority of people have normal sized hands.

Small

My wife, Julia, has small hands. She is quick to act and she's always looking at the bigger picture. She has great ability to organise large projects, but at times, finds herself with challenges with the finer details. Small handed people are independent thinkers who can visualise large scale plans and are open minded. They prefer to stay out of the lime light, and work behind the scenes. These people make great managers, events co-ordinators, salespeople, working in advertising and the practical and creative fields. They can get quite upset when things they didn't plan for, like minor details, get in the way of much larger plans.

THE QUALITY OF THE LINES

By looking at the palm, you can tell the quality of the line and its influence.

Deeply Cut

They denote strength in this aspect of the person's life. If it's the heart line, this person is passionate, loving and emotional. If it's the head line, this person substitutes as the ideal thinker and the mental aspect of their lives. When the life line is deeply cut, this person has a strong vitality of health and constitution. The depth of the line can give an indication of the time they enjoy the traits and qualities of the line, before something else in life challenges them, or becomes less important to them and the line weakens.

Thin

It's the opposite of the deeply cut line. Their strengths and qualities don't lie in this particular area of their lives.

Broad Shallow

There is only an average level of energy running through this particular line. It can be a sign of a decline of interest usually due to physical or emotional factors in one's life.

Normal

Has a nice depth to it and is pleasing to the eye. Through experience of looking at the lines, you will get to know the difference between deep, shallow, thin and normal lines. The normal line has an efficient amount of energy going through this aspect of the person's life. Giving them the experiences and the challenges that this line has to offer.

Apart from the major lines of the hand, heart, head and life, you will see tiny influence lines rising or descending or cutting through these major lines. They indicate their influence depending on the varying thicknesses of the lines, on the important moments in time for that person's life.

THE HAND SHAKE

Firm hand shake – this person is energetic, reliable and mature.
Weak hand shake – this person is restless, unsure of themselves, likes to worry and fret alot of the time.
Cold and clammy hand shake – This person is very sensitive, emotional and nervous. This shake can indicate a sign of poor health and constitution.
Strong grasp hand shake – this person is confident, energetic, reliable and dependable.

HOW MANY LINES ARE VISIBLE

Covered

This is called the full hand. The mind is always going and never shuts off. Their energy is scattered and need to focus their attention. They tend to live off excitable nervous energy. Usually found on sensitive hands, like the water hand, and they can be very creative and intuitive only when they can get their minds to focus and direct their energies to where they want to go. Meditation and yoga works wonders for these people. Most of the time they are highly strung, nervous types who are always on the go. Full handed people need to relax and let go, as the Beatles sang, "Let it Be."

Moderate

These people have a good amount of balance and energy in their lives. Being able to focus their talents, and skills in the right areas. The mind is relatively quiet, and they have a tendency to be goal-orientated and being practical.

Few lines

When there are only a few lines on the palm of the hand, it is called the empty hand. These people, depending on the shape and texture of their hand, can be sensitive and spiritual if the skin is soft and quite thick to touch. These people can be quite self-sufficient and be deemed as old souls.

If the skin texture is quite coarse, they can be quite methodical and straight forward in their approach to life. They do things in their own time and pace and can be seen quite cold, emotionally. As seen on the Earth hand.

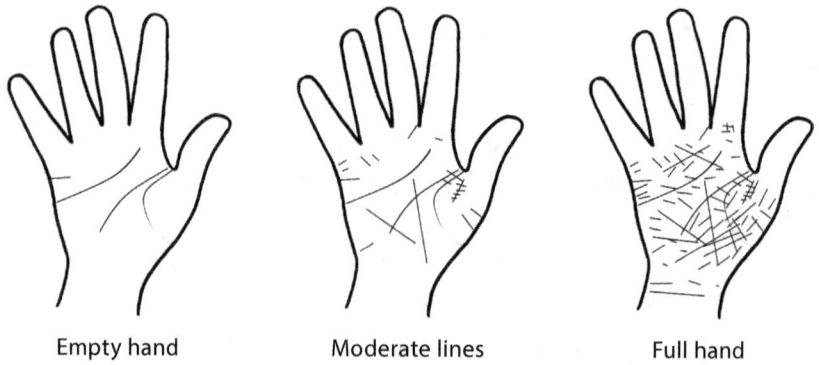

Empty hand   Moderate lines   Full hand

THE HAND SPREAD

Held close

When the fingers are held close together with no spaces in between the fingers, this person is a conformist. They show a traditional, conventional way of doing things. They are law-abiding and don't like to rock the boat. These people conform to the group, their peers and are creatures of habit and behaviour, they don't like change. Most of the time they can be seen as introverts, shy and don't like crowds.

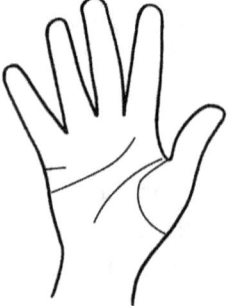

Held apart

When there are gaps between the fingers, these people can be seen as extroverts. They are independent to those around them, and like to think for themselves. Rebels and original thinkers, they have a good level of self-worth, enjoy relationships and life. They are always on the go and are stimulating to be around.

WHAT SHAPE

By looking at the shape of the hand you will be able to get a good idea of someone's character. You can get valuable insight into what your friend or client is like the first moment you greet them, before you even look at the palms of their hands.

The traditional hand shapes of palmistry can be divided into seven categories. These are the elementary, square, conic, spatulate, psychic, philosophic and the mixed hand. I am going to simplify this, and will be dividing the hands into four shapes based on the four astrological elements, fire, earth, air and water.

The first step is to look and measure the length of the palm. From the base of the fingers to the wrist. This indicates whether the palm is short or long.

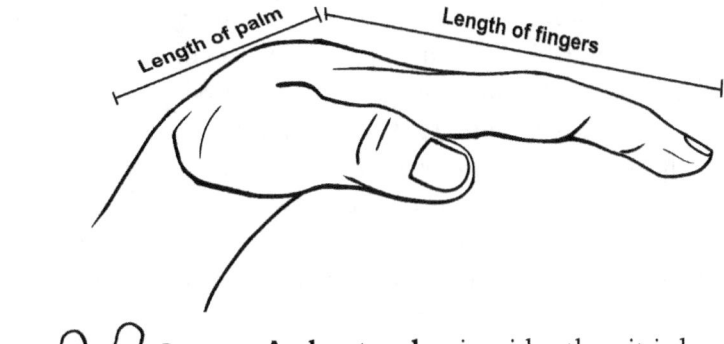

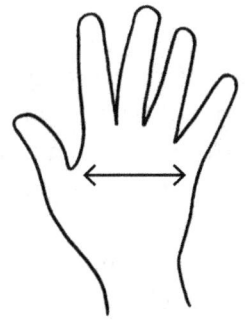

Width of palm

A short palm is wider than it is long.
A long palm is longer than it is wide.

Let's now see if the fingers are short or long. Measure the length of the palm, then the lengths of the fingers. If the fingers are shorter than the palm, or the same length, they are considered short. If the fingers are longer than the palm, they're considered long.

Determining the hand shape

Earth = Short square palm, short fingers and coarse skin.
Air = Short square palm, long fingers and paper skin.
Fire = Long narrow palm, short fingers and grainy skin.
Water = Long narrow palm, long fingers and silky skin.

THE EARTH HAND

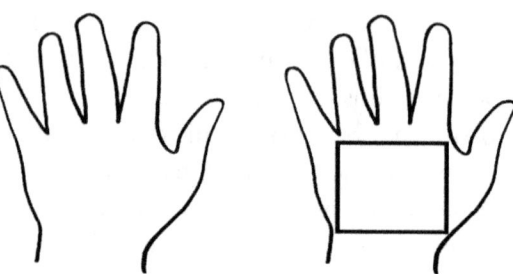

A short, square palm with short fingers is called the Earth hand. It is also known as the practical hand. The fingers are usually aligned at the top. These people like to get outdoors into the countryside. They enjoy nature, gardening and the feeling of the earth between their toes. They are the reliable ones in a group and someone to look to for advice. What you see is what you get with these people. Everything always has its place, they enjoy routine and plod around at their own pace. They dislike change, and love material security. If you are looking for a reliable employee, go for the person with the earth hand. They are always on time, dependable, hardworking and determined. They are in-tune with nature and are excellent at doing one activity at a time. You cannot rush these people.

When in love, common sense rules over their emotions, and they're not big on showing displays of affection. They're thorough, competent and careful with money. They prefer rules, methods and structures, and spontaneity is out of the question. Most of all, things have to be familiar, with rigid belief systems, otherwise things get a bit lost in transit.

The finger tips are often squarish, and so are the nails. Fingers and the thumb are usually firm and don't like to bend backward. Their palms are often hard and coarse, but occasionally, they are soft. I have seen Earth hands belong to an international medium, an engineer and the CEO of the fire service. Usually they have just a few simple lines, with arched or looped prints. Never read a long little (Mercury) finger on an earth hand, as you would on the average hand as it's a deception. All the fingers on the earth hand are the same length it's a trap, so just remember that.

THE FIRE HAND

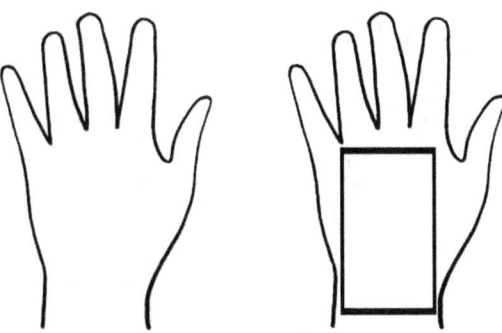

A long narrow palm with short fingers belongs to the fire hand. They're people who love adventure and are always on the go, seeking out new travels or what mountains to climb. They are impulsive and always seeking attention, they enjoy meeting new people and are spontaneous. They enjoy bush walking and smelling the fresh country air. Being on stage in front of an audience or leading, organising their employees of their own business suits them down to the ground.

They're people who tend to be always running off nervous energy, and can never settle down, having to be two steps in front of everybody else. They are impatient and need time out to let go and relax, otherwise they are prone to burnout. If they don't get the appropriate diet and sleep, they become short tempered and frustrated very early. When uptight, they will eat and drink to excess which is never a good combination. By learning to have a more balanced regime with the proper nutrition and exercise. Whatever they enjoy, this will counteract this, giving them the healthy lifestyle they require to remain balanced.

If you're looking for an energetic worker or friend, with plenty of enthusiasm and up for a challenge, look to the fire hand. They are competitive by nature and are always fun to be around, but they will probably wear you out.

There are not too many lines on this hand, only the major and some minor lines. The fingers are usually spatulate, with whorl fingerprints. The skin texture is usually quire firm, with a pinkish colour, giving them a healthy circulation.

THE WATER HAND

If you are looking at a hand that's long, with a long rectangular palm, with fingers that are as long or longer, than the palm, you're looking at a water hand. It can look like the hand has been stretched out, and the wrist will be small. These people are emotional, secretive, sensitive, creative and intuitive. But they are not practical, mowing the lawn and changing light bulbs are not their thing. Even more so, if their star signs are Cancer, Scorpio or Pisces. I have found their hands to be the most elegant and beautiful of all the hand shapes. Armed with great sensitivity, they can pick up on the atmosphere in a room or between two people quickly. They know when they are being lied to, so don't even try it. Unfortunately, due to their kindness and loving heart towards others, they can fall prey to other people's less than honest intentions, and be taken advantage of.

Most of the time, water hands feel like earth is a cruel and vicious place, and they don't belong here. Their imaginations are so great, they often drift off into other worlds as this one, can be seen as too harsh.

Water handed people are gentle and peace loving. They have good taste and refinement. They don't like to argue and if they feel defeated, they feel discouraged and go into themselves. It's the small things in life that matter to these people, and if you're competitive or have an ego, stay away, as they won't be interested. It's the mystical and the spiritual that gets their hearts beating faster, these people are passive, not assertive, so don't push them into anything they don't want to do. They can be influenced by people and circumstances and can't let go of something someone said years ago, so you must be careful with what you say. Unfortunately, they can become sponges for other people's problems and be disempowered quite easily.

They gravitate towards the helping and caring professions, such as animal rescue, hospitals, aged care homes, counselling and massage therapists. They also enjoy the arts because they are so creative and can be very good at painting, decorating, fashion design and modelling. Writing spiritual books or giving workshops on anything which brings meaning and purpose into other people's lives. Cooking and family are really important as well, and they make the greatest of friends. If you ever need a good friend to help you emotionally, they will be there at the drop of a hat to comfort you. They are so loyal, but don't betray their trust as they will never see you in the same light again.

Spiritual beliefs are very important to water hands, and I have seen many gifted clairvoyants and mediums with these hands. They believe there has to be more to life than the nine to five grind, and they're definitely right about that.

Usually, found on women, their hands are soft with many lines, including long vertical lines with loop type fingerprints. The long fingers they possess come with almond shaped nails. Meditation and going for walks in nature or along the beach are a great energy booster for water handed people, are a great way for them to enjoy the day, and play.

THE AIR HAND

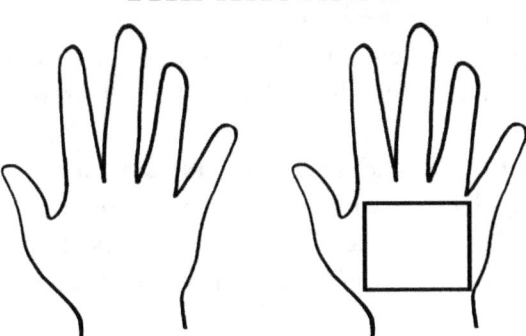

Air handed people have a square palm with long fingers. The skin has a dry feel to it, with rounded finger tips with loop fingerprints. These people are constantly in their heads. They are thinking, talking, acting, communicating ideas and information. They love to write novels, letters or in their diaries to get all this information down on paper.

They are always curious, about how things work, and how it all fits together. They enjoy discussions and conversations about what their latest ideas are, or something they've learnt or just heard about. Having their minds stimulated, a good conversation, book or crossword, just don't bore them with meaningless chatter.

These people are of a curious mind and love to study, but when it comes to the affairs of the heart, they tend to go with their heads and not their hearts. Over analysing every detail to death, which only makes matters worse; they tend not to experience emotions or feelings and would rather ask questions like, Why has this happened? What should I have done? or What did I not do to have this occur in my life?

If this sounds like you, get your journal out and let go of all your emotions and feelings onto paper to clear your head, and open your heart. Before you let the circumstances of your life disempower you. Writing it all down is a good way to release repressed emotional energy. Air handed people like the company of others who can stimulate their minds, especially in a partner. Otherwise they'll get bored, there must be adventure and not too much routine.

When it comes to employment the communication fields best suit them. From radio to television, journalism, writing for the local newspaper or interviewing people for magazines. I have also found teachers, lecturers at university, who have air hands as well. Being able to communicate information to students in their own unique style really appeals to them. The also enjoy the arts, theatre, paintings, music, literature and if they have sloping head lines, they're probably artists themselves.

The lines on their hands are clearly marked but are thin, not deep, like an earth hand. Fingers are flexible, but at times can have knuckles that appear swollen or thicker. This means they like to bounce around ideas and thoughts, discuss and debate before making any decisions, in their lives.

The hand

QUIZ TIME QUESTIONS

Time for a test to see what you've learnt and understood so far. What hand type are they?

1. Great at communicating
2. Sensitive and thoughtful
3. Spontaneous, but impatient
4. Likes to encourage and inspire
5. Lively and Inquisitive
6. Not really emotional or affectionate
7. Common sense rules their emotions
8. Influenced easily by others
9. Competitive by nature, always on the go
10. Love having their minds stimulated
11. Loves adventure
12. Enjoys routine and dislikes change
13. Spiritual and intuitive
14. Not interested in mindless chatter

Answers:

1. Air, **2**. Water, **3**. Fire, **4**. Fire, **5**. Air, **6**. Earth, **7**. Earth, **8**. Water, **9**. Fire, **10**. Air, **11**. Fire, **12**. Earth, **13**. Water, **14**. Air.

QUIZ TIME QUESTIONS

What have you learnt about their certain characteristics of the hand?

1. These people have poor circulation, what is the colour of the hand?
2. These people are dreamers, like using their imaginations, what is the texture of the palm?
3. These people have high energy and vitality, what colour are their hands?
4. These people love to debate and always have their heads in a book, what is the texture of the hand?
5. These people rarely have any energy and can be found indoors, what's the colour of their hands?
6. These people don't have too many friends and are always sick or have ill health, what's the texture of the hand?
7. These people have a cynical and depressive type of nature with an

excess of bile in the body, what's the colour of the hand?
8. These people have lost interest in life and enjoy introspection, what colour hands do they have.
9. These people are productive, conventional and practical, what's the texture of their palm?
10. These people will be mostly found in the communication fields of employment, what is the texture of their skin?
11. People with flexible fingers are adaptable   T/F
12. People who have stiff fingers are stubborn   T/F
13. People with long fingers are intellectual and into detail   T/F
14. Short fingered people are impulsive   T/F
15. Large handed people like to analyse and enjoy fine detail   T/F
16. Small handed people are quick to act   T/F
17. A hand with many lines is called _____?
18. A hand with a few lines is called _____?
19. Fingers that are held close together, this person is a _____?
20. Fingers that are held apart with gaps is an extrovert and a free thinker   T/F

Answers:

1. Blue, **2.** Soft and silky, **3.** Red, **4.** Paper bony hands with pronounced knuckles, **5.** White, **6.** Hard and thin, **7.** Yellow, **8.** White, **9.** Coarse, **10.** Paper, **11.** True, **12.** True, **13.** True, **14.** Impulsive, **15.** True, **16.** True, **17.** Full hand, **18.** An empty hand, **19.** Conformist, **20.** True.

FIVE

Fingers

*No one is free who has not obtained the empire of himself.
No man is free who cannot command himself.* — PYTHAGORAS

When you look at the fingers you're going deeper into the exploration of the psychological makeup of ourselves. When looking at your hand, or that of the person in front of you. Always observe when the hands are relaxed and still. This gives you a better judgment of the finger lengths, bends and gaps between the fingers.

LENGTH

Long fingers

Long

If the fingers are long and I mean as long as the palm of your hand, or longer, this is considered long. These people are very much into detail and at times like to over analyse, the nuts and bolts of a situation. They're thinkers and are very much in their heads than listening to their hearts. Being critical and pernickety about themselves and those around them, can be a flaw. Impatience and judgmental is a side to them that usually gets them into trouble. People with long fingers are seen as intellectuals and have a unique talent or a particular area that they specialize in, which makes them happy and fulfilled. I have seen many long fingered people who are also interested in spiritual pursuits, like meditation, yoga and self-development.

Short fingers

Not like their long finger counterparts, these people are quick and impulsive. They tend to go by instinct, following their hearts. Thinking for too long is just not them as they like to get on with things. So, at times they can be impatient, as well.

Long fingered people like to dwell in the abstract, short fingered people like to see the bigger picture when dealing with a situation.

Knotty fingers

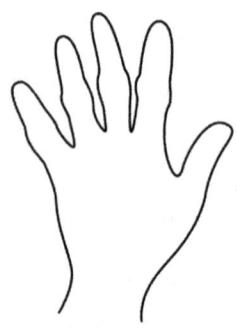

Knotty fingers

If you have knotty fingers or come across these, so the knuckles look swollen and are not suffering from arthritis. These are knotty fingers and those that have these love to think about things for a while. Bouncing ideas around in their minds before making any decisions is usual. I have found that most people who have knotty fingers like to debate and argue to get their point across. Most were on the debating team at school, due to their great argumentative talents. They respond well to reason and logic, and are independent, original thinkers. People who have these fingers make great debaters, scientists, philosophers and they love to play chess as well. Knotty fingers are the minority, where smooth fingers are more common.

Smooth fingers

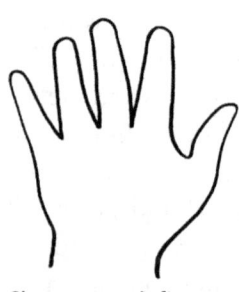

Short, smooth fingers

These people who have smooth fingers live in their hearts, using intuition rather than logic and reason. If you have smooth fingers, you are adaptable, sociable and like to go with the flow of life. People working in the caring professions, like doctors, nurses, alternative therapies such as massage, healing, artists and poets all have smooth fingers. The length or thickness of the three sections of the fingers, called the phalanges, can tell you about someone's personality.

Long top joint

Shows a thoughtful, caring person, but someone who likes to use their intellect as well. A quick note, if you notice a thickness to a finger which stands out among the rest, of the other fingers and is not affected by arthritis, this person is working with the strong qualities of the finger to their full effect, for instance, a thick index/Jupiter finger. This person will be self-assured, independent, a leader and may be quite religious.

Long middle joint

Shows a practical person who likes to manifest ideas into reality. They have a good business sense and make great business owners or entrepreneurs.

Long bottom joints

Show a material side to life. Lover of food, comfort or luxury, especially when the bottom joint is thicker. Eating to excess is usually the culprit here.

OTHER MARKINGS ON THE FINGERS

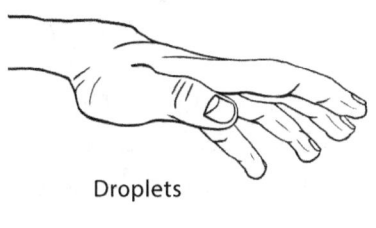

Droplets

Droplets

When there are droplets of skin on the fingertips, this person is sensitive to people and the environment around them. They are usually creative, artistic and most of the time very intuitive.

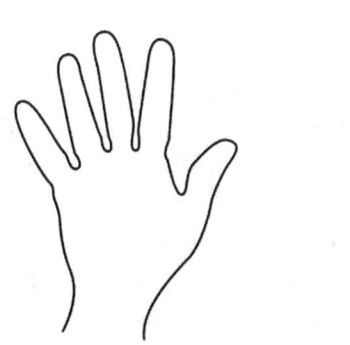

Pinched in fingers

Pinched in

When the bottom joint has a pinched in look, waisted look. This belongs to a self-disciplined eater and they like to have their lives and possessions in the right locations at all times, nothing needs to be out of place.

Fat pads

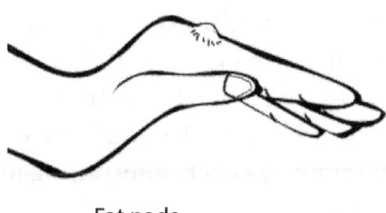

Fat pads

When there is an excess pad of flesh on the back of the third phalange, this person has a weight problem, usually since childhood. A good healthy eating plan and regular exercise keeps these people at the correct weight.

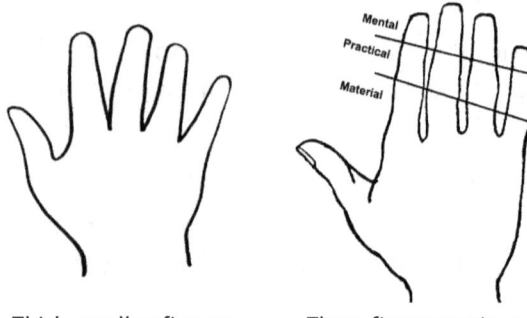

Thick, swollen fingers   Three finger sections

THE FINGERS INDIVIDUALLY

The index or Jupiter finger

The first finger, which is your index finger is called Jupiter. This finger relates to self-confidence, ambition and how self-sufficient you are. Do you like to take the lead or let someone else take charge and go with the flow?

Long Jupiter

Long

If it's straight and long, you're a very confident person, maybe a bit bossy or egotistical. You may like to delegate and be in charge at work or your social life. Most people I have met have strong religious opinions when the Jupiter finger is considered long. You definitely don't like being told what to do.

While I'm writing about the lengths of this finger, if Jupiter goes further than two-thirds of the way up to the top joint of the middle finger (Saturn), which is the closest, it's considered long. If it reaches only half way up or shorter than the ring finger (Apollo), which is on the other side of the middle finger (Saturn), it is considered short. The first and third fingers by average are usually the same length. Any differences between these two fingers and you will know, by sheer observation, if the index or Jupiter finger is long or short.

Short

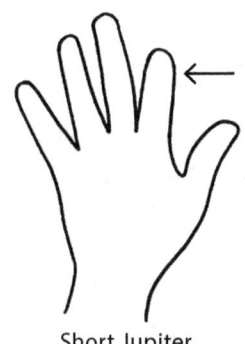

Short Jupiter

A short finger shows someone who feels insecure and not sure of themselves in life. They feel inferior and become followers. Sometimes they become tyrants to make up for their short index/Jupiter finger, and become dominating and loud. As children, short fingered index/Jupiters, weren't provided with reassurance from their parents, and at times, give away their power and control to longer fingered folk. Napoleon Bonaparte had a short index/Jupiter finger, just like his height. People who are short and have a short index/Jupiter finger, are often referred to as having a Napoleon complex.

Oddity

Twisted Jupiter

If the finger sticks out away from the middle/Saturn finger, this is a sign of the individual, a person who likes to think for themselves. Now if the finger twists towards the middle/Saturn finger, the bearer feels insecure and not sure of their self-worth, giving them the feeling of not having stability or security. The reason the index/Jupiter finger bends towards the middle/Saturn finger, is due the middle/Saturn finger being the finger of stability and security. Because of this twist, the owner will usually like to collect things to make up for their insecurities. People with a twisted index/Jupiter finger don't like to take risks and can be seen as shy and introverted.

The middle or Saturn finger

This is the middle finger and is the longest of the fingers most of the time. It reveals the serious side of our natures. Duty and responsibility to ourselves and others, getting ahead, dealing with money and real estate. Organisations, structure, power and male authority or male figures can be seen here or how you interact with these people in your own life.

Long

Long Saturn

If the finger is developed and long, the person will be serious, reliable and stable, always showing a great deal of duty and responsibility. At times this person may be told to lighten up, as they can be all work and no play. Making a life and not living a life, there is a difference. These people enjoy structure in organisation, or at work, and love the protocol of rules and regulations. At times, the long index fingered Saturnian, can get quite cynical and depressed if they don't enjoy themselves, or get their own way. They are very introspective and can enjoy their solitude.

Short

Short Saturn

But if it's short as the two fingers on either side of it are the same lengths. This person will be easy going, not caring about conformity, rules or regulations. Short fingered middle or Saturn people, are usually dropouts, misfits, and people who live an unconventional lifestyle. They don't like to hold a responsible job. They prefer to take the odd job when they need money.

The ring or Apollo finger

It is the third finger or ring finger. It represents our creativity, luck, artistic endeavours, taking risks, as well as a need for attention depending on its length. Apollo is the God of the arts, so when the finger is long, the bearer will be artistically talented in some way. It can be painting, drawing or acting. The finger is usually the same length as the index or Jupiter finger. But when considered long, it reaches past two-thirds of the top joint of the middle or Saturn finger.

Long

When the finger is considered long, usually more on males than females, the owner likes to have the spotlight on them. Check to see if they have a short index/Jupiter finger, most of the time they do. This is

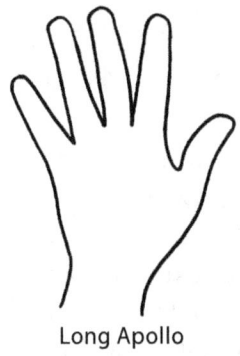
Long Apollo

because they are making up for low self-confidence and are in need of approval and validation, as it wasn't given at an earlier age by parents or peers. When a male has a long ring/Apollo finger, it has been proven by research that they have high levels of testosterone and are highly attractive to the opposite sex.

I have found that the celebrities that have seen me, men or women, have long ring/Apollo fingers. Now, if they're not artistic or creative in some way, they will show you what they have to offer, a nice house, a flashy car, jewellery or expensive clothes. These people like to take risks, whether it be gambling, a new business venture, or socially, whatever takes their fancy. This finger can also be called the peacock finger. Just like the peacock, it is all about the display and look at me with my beautiful feathers.

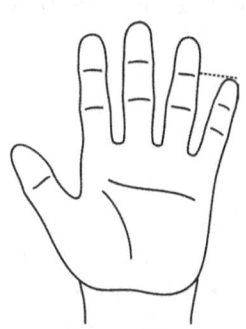
Normal Mercury

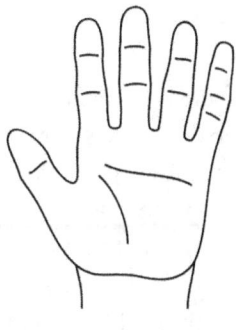
Long Mercury

The little or Mercury finger

Also known as the little finger, it reveals our communication skills, verbally or written, finance and sexual communication. To consider this finger to be short, long or average, check to see if it reaches to the first joint of the ring/Apollo finger. If it does it is considered to be average. If the little finger goes well beyond the first crease of the top phalange, it is considered long. When the finger is lowset, you have to add another half a centimetre to the length to give it it's appropriate length and meaning.

Long

When considered long, this person has a gift with words both orally and written, and they can communicate what they want to say with great effect. People with long little/Mercury fingers can be found as writers, lawyers, teachers, politicians and finance bankers. I have found them to be great at investing money, but very careful with where their money goes.

Short

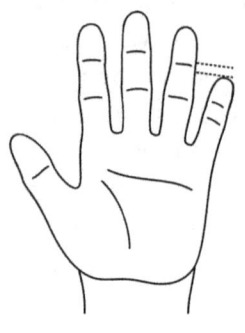

Short Mercury

Expressing oneself isn't one of the greatest of attributes for a short little/Mercury person. They often feel frustrated and misunderstood with what they want to express. Gaining a larger vocabulary through the reading of books and going to Toastmasters, will help a great deal with their self-confidence. People with short Mercury fingers tend to spend on impulse and buy items they don't need. Obviously they never save for a rainy day. A short Mercury finger can denote doing things on the dodgy as well. That's why most men in the Mafia subconsciously wear a ring on their little finger to balance out the shiftiness. It is a dead giveaway to a palmist. No pun intended.

Low set

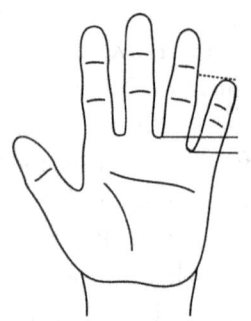

Low set Mercury

This is quite common more so on women, than men. Seven times more so, which relates to a parent not being there emotionally or physically which leads this person to sexual immaturity and having unconventional relationships with someone much older than themselves. They are looking to regain the mother or father relationship they never had growing up.

Bent

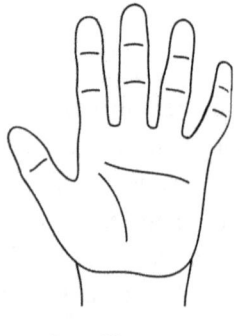

Bent Mercury

When the little finger bends towards the ring/Apollo finger, this person knows how to charm others through the use of words to get themselves out of trouble or get what they want out of life. It can also mean this person will do anything to help a friend in trouble, which may be seen as dishonest. The person who has a bend in their little finger most of the time, has a kind nature and can be taken advantage of.

This bending finger is called the wilt of sacrifice. Make sure you check all of the characteristics of the hand, like colour and texture of the palm, hand type and length of fingers before coming to a certain conclusion. Everything must be taken into consideration first, before coming to any conclusions with yourself or others.

Oddities of Mercury

Top joint thicker

If the top joint looks thicker or swollen, this person will be a great public speaker, or likes to talk for the sake of talking. They could talk under water, literally.

Two phalanges

If there are only two phalanges instead of the usual three, this person can be seen as someone who takes unusual risks. They may be regarded as different or unconventional and likes to do things a little bit shifty.

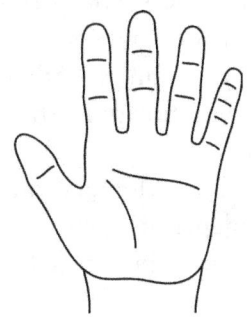

Mercury with 4 joints

Four joints

When the little/Mercury finger has four phalanges, this person is a great lover of words. Probably a writer and will enjoy speaking many different languages. I have only seen this on one person, who is an intelligent, gifted teacher and writer.

Middle phalange

If the middle phalange is shorter than the top and the bottom, this person doesn't like to organise their life and usually lives in an untidy environment, whether it is at work or at home. They can also have unconventional mannerisms and behaviour, that disturb those closest to them.

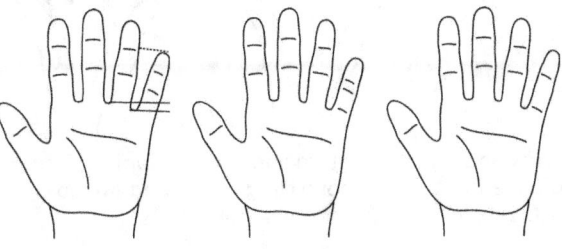

L - R:
Mercury normal position
Short middle joint
Mercury with 2 joints

FINGERS THAT CLING

When the index/Jupiter and middle/Saturn fingers bend towards the ring/Apollo finger, this person likes to follow their heart and listen to their intuition. The subconscious mind is more active than the conscious.

1. When the little/Mercury and ring/Apollo fingers lean toward the middle/Saturn, this means the subconscious mind wants to be channelled into reality. A very creative mind, with a good imagination, which is a great recipe for someone to manifest their dreams into reality.
2. When the middle/Saturn and ring/Apollo fingers cling together this person has had to give up on their dreams or aspirations for duty and responsibility. They are someone who is gifted with a particular talent but has taken a job for security, or having to look after a sick or elderly parent.
3. When the index/Jupiter, middle/Saturn and ring/Apollo fingers cling together, this person is sensitive and feel like they can't make it on their own, so they become dependent on others. They need people around them and belong to a group for reassurance.
4. When the little/Mercury and ring/Apollo fingers cling together, this person wants more action, adventure and authority in their lives, but they don't know how to go about it.
5. When the middle/Saturn, ring/Apollo and little/Mercury fingers cling together, this person wants to be independent and ambitious. They waste time in areas which won't contribute to what they want in life.
6. When the index/Jupiter and middle/Saturn fingers cling together, this person suffers from poor self-confidence, but they really have the talent and ability if they put the effort in.

Jupiter and Saturn bend towards Apollo

Mercury and Apollo bend towards Saturn

Saturn and Apollo cling together

Jupiter, Saturn and Apollo cling

Fingers

Mercury and Apollo cling together   Saturn, Apollo and Mercury cling together   Jupiter and Saturn cling together

LET'S LOOK AT THE GAPS

A gap between:

Gap between Jupiter / Saturn

The index/Jupiter and middle/Saturn fingers

This person has an independent shape of mind. They like to think for themselves and is a free thinker. These people make great leaders, managers, business magnates and love to be self-employed. Making decisions for other people is one skill they have, without the interference or pressures from those around them.

Gap between Saturn / Apollo

The middle/Saturn and ring/Apollo fingers

These people can be seen as quite ambitious and domineering. They like to know it all, which gets them into trouble with work colleagues and friends alike. They tend to live in the moment and not care too much about the future, usually brought on by a serious illness that they had and got over. Most of the time they have trust issues so people have a hard time connecting with them, which puts people off and keeps them away.

The ring/Apollo and little/Mercury fingers

This person likes to do things their own way, they are independent of action. They can usually be a little bit eccentric and they don't like to conform to what is expected of them. This makes them a joy to be around. Sexual promiscuity while they are in relationships is quite common. Especially when the little/Mercury finger is long, a large Mount of Venus is present, as well as a Girdle of Venus, and coarse texture of the palm. There are two sides to this person and only a few may know the real side. Most of the time when there is a space here, the person is going through sexual difficulties or have unconventional thoughts or actions between sex and relationships. I have seen this spacing on many people who have had affairs.

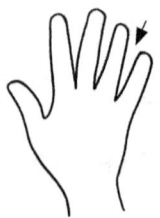 

Normal spacing between Apollo / Mercury   Wide spacing between Apollo / Mercury

All gaps

When there are gaps between all of the fingers, this person is an extrovert, they are excitable enthusiastic and enjoy a challenge. At times they can be seen as a non-conformist as they enjoy living their life differently to others.

No gaps

When the fingers are all held in close, with no spacings, this person is a conformist, who doesn't like to rock the boat and is a team player.

Extrovert spacing between fingers   A conformist hand, limited spacing between fingers

WHAT DO THE TOPS OF THE FINGER TIPS LOOK LIKE

Square

When the tops of the fingers are square, these people are methodical. They can be quite precise, practical and efficient in what they do.

Round

When the tops of the fingers are round, these people are just your average run of the mill people, who are easy going and are team players.

Spatulate

When the tops of the finger are thicker, these people love the outdoors, like adventure, most often like sport, and can be quire entrepreneurial. They like to invest in businesses and new ways of doing things. They need solid evidence before they see your point of view.

Pointed

These tops are found on sensitive people, psychics and artistic folk alike. They live in an ideal world, and cannot tolerate loud people, environments, alcohol or drugs, as they are all too damaging to their emotional and mental energies.

QUIZ TIME QUESTIONS

What have you learnt about the fingers

1. If a child's parent was missing emotionally or physically, what sign would be on their hand?
2. If you are a great communicator, what finger would be long?
3. Some who is extroverted would have…
4. If you were creative and have artistic ability, what finger would be long?
5. If you are an independent thinker, where would the spacing be?
6. What type of fingers would you have if you like to debate and bounce around ideas, before making a decision?
7. If you have a feeling of insecurity, what finger would be short?
8. If you are a lover of neat and tidy work, and are methodical, what finger tips would you have?
9. If you were a lover of food and comfort, what bottom phalanges would you have?

Answers:

1. A low-set little/Mercury finger, **2.** Little/Mercury finger, **3.** Widely spaced fingers, **4.** Ring/Apollo finger. **5.** A space between the index/

Jupiter and the middle/Saturn fingers, **6.** Knotty fingers, **7.** Index/Jupiter finger, **8.** Square tipped fingers, **9.** Thick and fat bottom phalanges.

THE FINGERPRINTS

Palmistry is all about discovering who we are, what we're good at and what we can improve on. By looking at the prints on the pads of your fingertips, we can go into deeper detail on how we process information that we receive and act on, depending on what prints we have on a particular finger. This information will add to your in-depth analysis and insight into understanding yourself, and others.

The scientific name for the study of fingerprints is Dermatoglyphics, which is Greek for skin carvings. Although over time, the lines on your hands may change, the prints on your fingerprints don't. By learning the different types of fingerprints you'll get the unchangeable element of your character.

There are five main types of prints

The Loop

Radial loop

Ulnar loop

This is about fitting in and being a team player. They like to belong to a group. These prints are very common and can be seen as average. There are two types of loops, Ulnar being the most common, the print is turning away from the thumb.

The Radial loop print begins towards the thumb side. Radial loops are on people who are very open and sensitive. These people aren't sure of themselves. They're really friendly and always put other people's needs before their own. The radial loop is most often found on the passive, non-dominant hand before the age of twenty-one.

The Whorl

This is the mark of an individual, the opposite of a loop. They like to think for themselves and come up with original ideas and like to be different in some way. They always have a skill that they master, always focused and they love their freedom. My beautiful wife, Julia, has many whorl prints, on her fingers and one of the reasons we are together. She's an individual and likes to think and act for herself, like her husband, I guess.

The Arch

When I think of the arch, I think of my brother-in-law. He's practical, always working on something with his hands and can be quite stubborn at times. He always get stuck in old patterns on how things use to be. He is inventive, highly motivated and enjoys good old values from yesteryear.

Composite

These prints are actually two loops going in opposite directions. They find it hard to make up their minds, seeing two points of view and always seeing two sides of every story. Many counsellors and lawyers have these prints on their fingertips, as they are always open to discuss other ways of doing things. This ability will bring about a better outcome for their clients.

Tented Arch

This pattern is just like the arch pattern, but has a peak at the top of the arch that goes to a point. They like to take everything to an extreme, are very enthusiastic with everything they do. It's a rare print.

THE MAIN CHARACTERISTICS OF EACH PRINT PATTERN

Loop
Positives: adaptable, easy-going, sociable.
Negatives: people pleaser, lose their sense of self.

Whorl
Positives: individual, original, gifted.
Negative: egotistical.

Arch
Positives: practical, reliable, loyal.
Negative: stubborn.

Composite
Positives: open minded, sees two sides to every story.
Negative: indecisive.

Tented Arch
Positives: enthusiasm, excitable.
Negative: fanatical.

QUIZ TIME QUESTIONS

What have you learnt about the fingerprints

1. People with loops, are they individuals or team players?
2. A person with a lot of whorls, are they gifted and original in some way?
3. What print gives the gift of being able to enjoy working with one's hands?
4. If a person has composite prints do they make up their minds easily?
5. What loop would I have if I put others' needs before my own?
6. What's a negative trait of a person with arch prints?
7. What's a positive trait of a person with composite prints?
8. What is the rarest print?
9. What's the most common print?
10. Would a person with a tented arch, be dull and boring?

Answers:

1. Team players, **2.** Yes always, **3.** Arches, **4.** No indecisive, **5.** Radial loop, **6.** Stubborn, **7.** Open minded, **8.** Tented arches, **9.** Ulnar loop, **10.** No they're very enthusiastic and excitable.

WHAT FINGERPRINTS MEAN ON THE FINGERTIPS THEMSELVES

Any small differences between the fingerprints, will also indicate a difference in the character. Let's look at the individual fingers, with different fingerprints.

Loops have not been added here, as they are too commonly occurring to write about. Remember, people with loops are easy going, reliable people who conform and are sociable. Unfortunately, they are not unique enough to discuss here, apart from the radial loop.

Radial loop

A radial loop is usually found on the index/Jupiter finger, and this person is considered very shy and insecure. Who needs to be encouraged, they're very sensitive and have trouble dealing with critical and loud obnoxious people. They have a gift of understanding people and are able to tune into the atmosphere around them to see whether it is hostile or friendly. They always put the needs of others, before their very own as they feel they are not worthy. Due to this feeling, always looking for reassurance from those around them. This stems from a childhood where the environment was very hostile and encouragement was absent.

The radial loop is always found on the non-dominant hand, before the age of twenty-one, the childhood years. I have this print here and through working on myself have changed through inner-transformation. My dominant index/Jupiter finger, now carries the ulnar loop pattern, which describes someone who has worked hard, through earlier difficulties to become the person they wanted to be.

INDEX/JUPITER FINGER

This is the finger of self, it outlines your confidence, ambition, self-esteem, leadership and what vision you have for yourself.

Whorl

You're an individual, have original ideas and insights. You like to do things differently, usually on your own, with a strong sense of self and most of the time they are self-employed.

Arch

You are a practical, cautious person, like to accomplish your own personal interests. Loyalty means a lot to you, and you find it difficult to change.

Tented Arch

You're enthusiastic and excitable about your interests, ideas and what you want to do. You can be seen as a motivator. Meditation is a great way of relaxing for this person as they can become too serious and highly strung.

Composite

You find it hard to stick to one belief, idea or attitude and goals. You can be easily influenced by other people, rather than yourself. Uncertainty of who you are and what you want is quite common with this print on the index/Jupiter finger.

THE MIDDLE/SATURN FINGER

This is the finger of duty and responsibility. The serious side to us in authority, lifestyle, business and values.

Whorl

On the second finger gives you a unique way of doing things in business. Working in a different job to others or achieving balance with your values, lifestyle than those around you. They dislike dogma and choose freedom over rules and regulations, and a non-traditional spiritual path suits you best.

Arch

You like to work in a practical aspect of employment, working with your hands outdoor work suits you better than being stuck in an office. You are very methodical in your approach with a good sense of fairness and old fashioned values.

Tented Arch

This fingerprint indicates that you're enthusiastic in whatever you do in work, or life in general. You like to do everything the right way, or not at all. Can be a perfectionist and quite self-critical at times. Patience can be a challenge.

Composite

A composite print here means you are never sure if your job is the right one for you. You may change jobs quite often and can be quite undecided where you stand in your values and religion.

RING/APOLLO FINGER

This is the finger of creativity, artistic endeavours, risk taking and putting ourselves in a favourable light to those around us. Happiness and inner contentment can be seen in the Apollo finger.

Whorl

A whorl here indicates someone who is very creative has a good eye for originality, line, colour and form. They have their own unique style.

Arch

Someone who will work practically with their creative artistic side. I have found they enjoy sculpting with wood or clay. Painting with water colours whatever they like to do, it will be done with their hands, building chess pieces, charcoal drawings, carved wood boxes. These people are truly gifted.

Tented Arch

Will be found on the person who is enthusiastic excitable about special forms of art and their creativitiy. They will go to extreme lengths to put their work on display and have it seen by everyone who appreciates what they have to offer.

Composite

Shows someone who can have many creative outlets but never be a master of one, as they can't make up their mind of which avenue to take.

LITTLE/MERCURY FINGER

This is the finger for communication, written, verbal, sexual and finance. It is the way we express ourselves and the way we go about it.

Whorl

When a whorl is found here, the person has a very different way of expressing themselves from the ordinary, a gifted writer who has an unconventional intimate relationships with people. These people can also have very strong intuitions and premonitions, which can be quite vivid and very accurate. If you are one of these people, it would be a good idea to express what you see to those that require your knowledge and foresight.

Arch

This person may enjoy the complexities of speech and writing. They will be careful in what words they use in a sentence or getting their point across in a conversation.

THE THUMB

This has got to do with the strength of someone's character. It can be seen as the rudder of someone's life and how they manoeuvre themselves through life. They can be forceful, or diplomatic or going with the flow and making few waves.

Whorl

If a whorl print is seen here, you will have a unique method of going about life in your own original way. You will like to demonstrate your freedom and independence.

Arch

This indicates someone who is very practical, when going about what has to be done in their lives. At times, they can be quite stubborn, holding their ground and enjoying methodical and repetitive actions.

Composite

One minute their minds are made up to do something one way, and all of a sudden, they do it completely differently. Procrastination and giving into resistance usually occurs. Being very unpredictable is common when a composite print is found here, which at times gets everyone around them frustrated and annoyed.

QUIZ TIME QUESTIONS

What have you learnt about the prints on individualised fingers

1. If there is a whorl on the index/Jupiter finger, does this make the person an individual or a team player?
2. If you have a simple arch on the middle/Saturn finger, would you work in an office, or be more suited outdoors?
3. If you have a tented arch on the ring/Apollo finger, would you be enthusiastic, excitable and pleased to display your art?
4. If you have a whorl on the thumb, would you do things in a different unique way than those around you?
5. If you have a composite print on your index/Jupiter finger, would you find it hard to stick by your goals and what you want for yourself?
6. What kind of print would you have on the index/Jupiter finger, if you are a motivator of people?

7. If you have a whorl print on the little/Mercury would you be intuitive?
8. If you have a radial loop on your index/Jupiter finger, would you put your needs before others?
9. If you had a composite on the middle/Saturn finger, would you know from a very young age what you wanted to do for a job?
10. Would you play by your own rules if you had a whorl on the middle/Saturn finger?

Answer:

1. An individual, **2.** Outdoor Employment, **3.** Yes, **4.** Yes, **5.** Yes, **6.** Tented Arch, **7.** Yes, **8.** Yes, **9.** No, **10.** Yes.

SIX
The Thumb

> If there were no other evidence of the existence of God, the thumb
> is a symbol of the divine aspect of man. — *ISAAC NEWTON*

Want to know the character and driving force in your life? Look no further than your thumb. This is the rudder of your life and how you move through it. Do you push your way to the top, climbing the ladder of success, getting what you want? Willpower, determination and sound logic are the main ingredients seen in the big, strong thick thumb.

Or maybe you have a small weak looking thumb, that doesn't look right on the hand. Giving you no willpower to strive for goals or vision that you see for yourself. Unfortunately there is never enough energy and enthusiasm to keep people interested in what they want to pursue. Most of the time they lack the self-confidence and surety, as their large thumbed counterparts.

Big, strong, thick thumb   Small thumb

The long and short of it

To determine how long your thumb is, move the thumb alongside the first finger which is called Jupiter. Now if the top of the thumb reaches halfway of about the bottom joint of the index/Jupiter finger, it's considered long. But if the thumb doesn't get to half way, it is considered short.

Long

If your thumb is considered long, you'll have a strong sense of self. The ego is healthy and getting one's way could be a priority. You are a doer, preferring action to daydreams. Turning dreams into a reality can be common, as ambition and determination are in plentiful supply. You like to be first in everything you do. You can be quite domineering, but you are a natural born leader.

Short

When considered short, you'll like to procrastinate and not have the drive to get what you want. At times throughout your life, opportunities will slip by due to not being willing to make any decisions. Because of this you can become frustrated and have bursts of anger due to not getting what you want out of life. By channelling your anger into the direction you want to move in, life will become a lot easier for you.

Medium

So, when the thumb is of medium length, half way up on the third joint of the index/Jupiter finger, you have a good balance between willpower and logic. This is enough for you to create the life you have envisioned for yourself. Making decisions depends on how much energy is available and how one's feeling in the moment. The ego is balanced and when needed you can rest when you feel like you should.

THE ANGLE OF THE THUMB

Closed

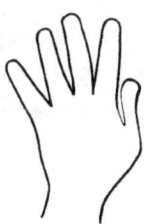

When the thumb is held close to the fingers, with no gap between the thumb and fingers, this is called a closed angle.

These people like to keep to themselves and not divulge anything about who they are and what's going on in their lives. By nature, they can be seen as stingy, secretive and cautious with not the ability to show any signs of affection at all. Usually seen as introverts, more interested in themselves with not much ambition at all. Most of the time people around them see them as cold fish.

Normal

When the thumb forms an angle around 45 degrees, this is considered normal. This person has a good balance when enjoying life, open, friendly and adaptable. They have the ability to pursue goals as they have energy available to stick to a ready-made plan, and see it through to completion.

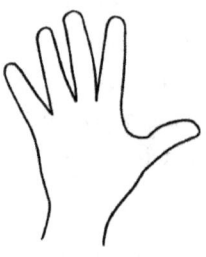

Wide

Now if the angle of the thumb is wider than 90 degrees, this is a wide open hand. The owner of this hand is generous, adaptable to life's situations and challenges. They have great willpower, discipline and motivation to lead people as they generally love to make the most out of everything they do. At times they can be seen to push the limits at what they can take on. A downside to the wide angle is people tend to take advantage of people with a wide angled thumb. They have to be aware of the people they surround themselves with. The wide angle thumb in palmistry is also called the Angle of Generosity.

WHERE IS THE THUMB SET?

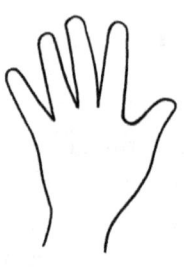

High

When the thumb is set high next to the fingers, these people can be seen as quite revered. They are more logical, and analytical, with their heads ruling their hearts.

Low

Now if the thumb is set low near the wrist, these people can be seen as more open, friendlier and generous. They are people's people. They like to play well with others, and enjoy socialising, meeting new people and facing life's challenges. They like to go with instinct over intellect.

When studying the thumb, always look at the length, width and overall thickness to get a great understanding of what type of thumb you have.

Length

This tells you how hard you try to get what you want, and put yourself out for others, and test your limits and boundaries in life.

Width

This tells you how much you will push and shove to get what you want. Will you try and manipulate and control things, or go with the flow in life?

Thickness

This show you how tactful or tactless you are, when expressing yourself and going after what you want. Are you pushy or diplomatic in the way you go about things?

THE FIRST JOINT — AMBITION AND WILLPOWER

So, if it's longer than the second joint, there is much willpower and determination with this person. They like to get their own way, and can be seen as quite ambitious. But, if it's too long, this person will always be in conflict with others. They can create dramas around them due to not wanting to compromise. At their worst, they are stubborn and hard-headed.

Shorter than second joint

Logic and reason will guide this person throughout their life. Ambition and willpower comes second to this person, as they like to think about things first, before making any decisions. These people are more pleasant to have around compared to someone who has a long first joint.

Two joints same length

Balance is in place here, and willpower and logic work as a team. They have the ability to make good decisions for all concerned, not just themselves.

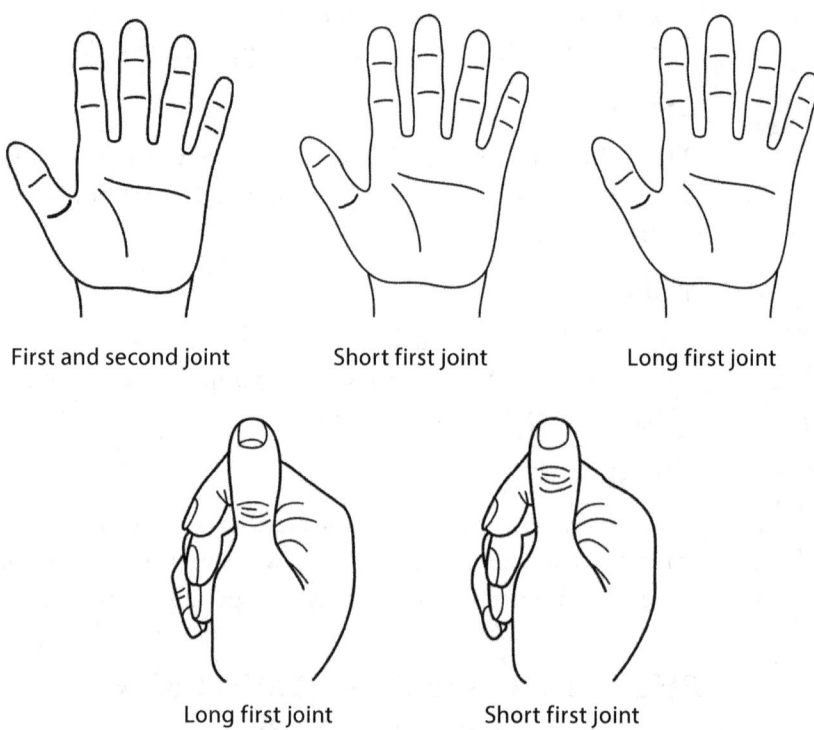

First and second joint   Short first joint   Long first joint

Long first joint   Short first joint

THE SECOND JOINT — LOGIC AND REASON

Long second joint — with a short top joint

If you have this thumb, you like to talk and think about what you are going to do, but have trouble getting around to doing it due to having a short top joint, and this shows a lack of willpower. Willpower gives us the enthusiasm to create in life.

Waisted or pinched in

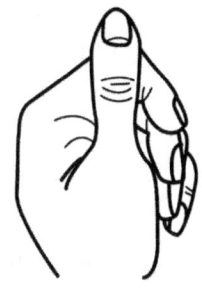

This is called the waisted thumb. People who have this, are friendly and go by their feelings when dealing with others. They use tact and diplomacy. They always act and think about others before making decisions. They make great managers and friends, and know how to get the best out of you.

Thick bottom joint

Being focused on the main objective, these people can be quite tactless and forceful when dealing with others. At times, they can rub people up the wrong way with what they say, as they have a limited mental filter.

Swollen thumb

If the thumb looks a lot larger than usual, especially around the top joint, these people tend to have fits of rage and anger. Unfortunately, they repress their emotions and frustrations. Not being able to express themselves in a productive way, they are like a kettle just waiting to boil. I was once coming back from London, and I was sitting next to a lady with this type of thumb. She asked me what I did for a living, and before I knew it, her hands were in my face, with her swollen thumb nearly poking me in the eye. When I explained to her about the type of thumb she had, you could have cut the air with a knife. She looked at her husband, and her husband looked at me, they quickly looked away. I wonder who wears the pants in that family. In times gone by, this thumb was called the Murderer's Thumb. As the people who have these thumbs had committed more murders than anybody else, back in Victorian times, as the legend goes.

Flat and squared

If you have a flat, tapered thumb, around the top joint, you can be impulsive when making decisions, and always having five things going on at once, and never completing any of them. I have a client who reads five books at a time and never finishes one of them, and then will start a new one. These people run on nervous energy. If you have a flat thumb tip, it is best to do one thing at a time, and focus on what you are doing now, instead of getting too far ahead of yourself. Meditation will work wonders for you. It will quieten your mind and bring your attention back to awareness of your present task.

LINE OF FRUSTRATION

First joint

Horizontal lines on the first joint of the thumb refer to your will. You don't know how to go about what you want to do, so you express frustration, sometimes out of procrastination or too much resistance from outside distractions and circumstances.

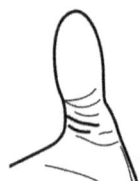

Second joint

Horizontal lines on the second joint have to do with being frustrated with our thinking. Not being able to come up with an answer to a problem or a solution to a challenge or obstacle that is creating difficulty in our lives.

Angle of the thumb

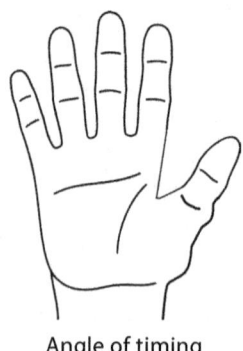

Angle of timing

If the joints of your thumb are prominent when you look at the palm of your hand, this is called the angles of the thumb. You'll have the gift of timing and rhythm. Many drummers have these angles, as well as sports people such as golfers and tennis players, because they require such excellent hand eye co-ordination. I have also seen it in many people who are dancers who can feel the beat and rhythm when moving with the music.

THE TIPS OF THE THUMB

Square

Round

Spatulate

Pointed

Curves back

If your tip curves back, you're quite charismatic, with a lot of personal magnetism. You enjoy life to the fullest, have a general concern for others, but have to stand out from the crowd. Has the thought ever crossed your mind, that you'll be famous one day.

Pointed

This person is idealistic, creative and intuitive.

Square

This person is practical, methodical, has old style values and can be seen as stubborn.

Round

People with rounded thumb tips are sociable, adaptable, have good reasoning skills, and have great balance between their thoughts and feelings. These people like to belong and go with the flow of life.

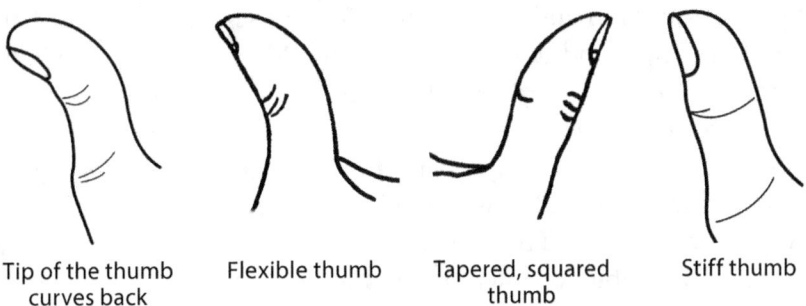

Tip of the thumb curves back   Flexible thumb   Tapered, squared thumb   Stiff thumb

DOES THE THUMB BEND?

The majority of people can say they have all the willpower and determination in the world, but by checking to see how flexible the thumb is, this will give you a great indication of if they walk their talk. Life is all about action. Action and effort equals results in our lives.

The quickest and easiest way to check how flexible the thumb is, is to gently pull back with your index/Jupiter finger slowly towards the wrist.

Supple jointed thumb

When the thumb is easy to pull back, the thumb is flexible, just like their personalities. They are easy to get along with, interesting and entertaining. Being distracted by those around them comes easily, as they can be seen as carefree, spontaneous and are always looking for distractions. They are much better when working in teams, or with a couple of friends, as they enjoy support to help them keep focussed on the current goal. They are quick to say yes to someone, but usually go back on their word, due to being in the moment, their kind nature or just being somewhere else within their mind. They are easily controlled by more domineering stiff thumb people. If you want to know who wears the pants in a relationship, have a glance at the thumb. Your boss will probably have a stiff jointed thumb, which is much larger and thicker than their partners.

Stiff jointed thumb

They can be quite domineering characters who resist everything and find it hard to make friends easily. They're not flexible, just like their thumbs and push through life with effort and determination. If you ask them a question and they say no, it's because there is nothing in it for them. Rigid and down the line is how they operate, and when it comes to patience, they don't have any, not compared to a person with a flexible thumb. You most definitely can't push them around and will answer you when they're good and ready. Adaptability to people and life's ups and downs aren't one of their strong points and they usually burn out. They burn the candle at both ends, and they need to find a hobby or interest that will help them relax and let go and not be so serious all the time. Meditation springs to mind.

QUIZ TIME QUESTIONS

What have you learnt?
1. Is it better to have a flexible thumb than a stiff thumb?
2. What does the thumb tell you about a person?
3. Is a stiff thumb person flexible and easy going?
4. How do you measure the thumb?
5. When the thumb is close to the hand, is this person open and friendly, or cold and withdrawn?
6. What does the first joint tell us about a person?
7. What does the second joint tell us about a person?

8. If the thumb is easy to pull back, what does this mean?
9. If the thumb is rigid and firm, what does this tell us about the person?
10. When the thumb has a pinch waisted look, what does this tell you about the person?

Answers:

1. Most definitely, flexible thumb people are easy going, enjoy life and are flexible with life. **2.** They have strength of character, willpower, determination, logic and reasoning abilities. **3.** No, they are strong headed and like to get their own way. **4.** By placing the thumb alongside the index/Jupiter finger and looking where the tip of the thumb reaches to. **5.** This person may be cold and withdrawn, they like to keep their cards close to their chests. **6.** Willpower and determination and how much they have. **7.** Logical reasoning ability when dealing with people and life in general. **8.** This person is carefree, relaxed, flexible and spontaneous. **9.** This person is very determined, stubborn and at times can be seen as quite domineering. **10.** Has great emotional intelligence. Likes to use tact and get the best out of people. They are always looking for a win-win solution.

SEVEN

Major Lines

Know thyself and all will be revealed — *PAMELA THERESA LOERTICHER*

HEART LINE

How do you love? Are you affectionate or do you like to play it cool. Can you express the way you feel? Do you see yourself as the dominant partner, or do you like to be passive and show your displays of affection in more subtle ways. It's here where we can find out all the answers to these questions and much more. Just by looking at your heart line. The heart line is located directly under the fingers and comes in two different forms, either curved or straight and long or short.

Curved

Now if your heart line is curved and moves up between the middle/Saturn and index/Jupiter fingers, you like to demonstrate your love and affection for friends, loved ones and partner. Hugs, kisses, holding hands, touching or being touched by those you admire is important. You're affectionate, warm and emotional when it comes to love, very much a hands on person, and you don't care who is looking. The physical approach to sex is essential for you and you most probably play the dominant role in your relationships. Being demonstrative, passionate, romantic and expressive are a definite when it comes to affections of the heart for you.

Straight

If you've got a straight heart line, you play a much more passive role not through affectionate kisses and embraces. But kind words, thoughtfulness and the connections which matter most to you of heart and mind. Displays of affection are left behind closed doors, not for all to see out in public and are much cherished when in private. The longer the line, the more the person responds to others. The shorter the line, the more introverted, selfish, closed off someone is to true love.

Heart line ending between Jupiter and Saturn

Straight heart line

POSITIONING OF THE HEART LINE

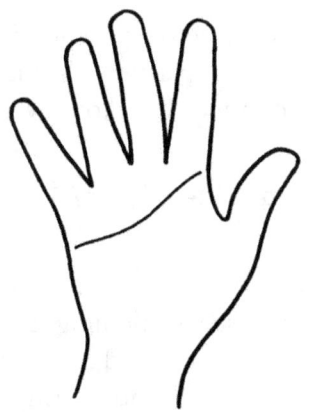
Heart line ending under Jupiter

Curved line under index/Jupiter finger

When the curved heart line ends under the index/Jupiter finger, this person knows exactly what they want in a partner. They can be quite fussy and wait for the right partner to come along. But they must have the right credentials. Most of the time, their partners become idolised, thinking they are better than they actually are, as if they have love coloured glasses on and don't see their faults. But when they do, this cuts very deeply and become very disappointed. People with this heart line, don't like to settle for second best, and usually marry later on in life after many relationships and disappointments.

This type of heart line demands a lot from their partner, sometimes more than what they can give. By remembering we are all human, and we have faults of our own, life and love will run a lot smoother. Don't put so many demands and commands on your partner and friends, they are humans and will make errors of judgement and mistakes. Balance is the key here because nobody is perfect, although the curved heart line under the index/Jupiter finger tend to think so.

Heart line ending between Jupiter and Saturn

Curved heart line between the index/Jupiter and middle/Saturn fingers

This is a great heart line to have, and people with this line have the balance of right idealism on one side of the coin and practical, reliable on the other. Their relationships tend to last because they put focus on their partners as well as looking after their own emotional needs as well. Most of the time the bearers of this line are happy and affectionate and will sacrifice parts of themselves for those they care about, as they know good relationships are all about give and take. They don't put their partners through anything they wouldn't do themselves. I have found them to be very wise beyond their actual years.

Curved heart line under Saturn

Curved line under the middle/Saturn finger

This person can be very forward and blunt when they see something they desire. They need physical and romantic satisfaction. Their sexual nature can be seen as aggressive, selfish, cold and reserved in the way they go about getting what they want. Emotional encounters with these people are cold without any tenderness whatsoever. With this particular heart line, it is their way or the highway, and if you don't fit in with what they want or operate, they gladly show you the door. Very unsentimental, with no regard for feelings for what they may want apart from what they have in mind for you.

Major lines

Long line underneath the index/Jupiter finger or longer

Longer heart line ending under Jupiter

Now, if you come across someone who has a straight heart line, that reaches underneath the index/Jupiter finger, or to the end of the palm, this person is definitely a humanitarian, who wants to help and love everyone accordingly. They are usually found working in missions overseas, charities, doctors, and care workers of some sort. They also like to work and live in communities that have the same values and principles as they do. They devote their time for the greater good, and people belonging to church families often have this line.

There can be a drawback here with this line if the balance isn't right. They can give too much to everyone and not enough to themselves, neglecting their emotional needs. If you have this long heart line, make sure to look after yourself first, paying attention to getting enough sleep, a proper healthy eating plan and time out for yourself. Otherwise, you may not be able to provide the love and care you wish to provide for those you care about.

Short, straight line under Apollo

Very short line

When the heart line ends under the ring/Apollo finger, the person will be sexually motivated, and is not interested in deep and meaningful relationships. They like to keep their interests at a sexual, physical level, without the emotional attachments.

Two or more branches

When the heart line has two or more branches at the end of the heart line, this shows there are many sides to their loving nature. One line ending between the index/Jupiter and the middle/Saturn fingers, and the other on the index/

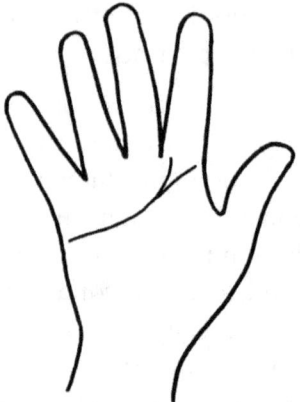 

Two branches off the heart line   Three branches

Jupiter finger. So, these people are romantic and demonstrative, but also thoughtful and understanding as well. The whole package really. But remember this, the more branches one has, the more complex their emotional needs will be for their partner and those around them.

Three or more branches

The most lucky sign of all is the heart line with three or more branches. These people require physical, emotional and mental stimulation when it comes to love. They're demonstrative, thoughtful and have love for all they meet. They have a great understanding of all the people, which makes them quite popular with everybody. This is due to their loving, nurturing nature. People with this heart line do well in life as they know how to get the best out of everyone they meet, and always leave a terrific impression.

Heart line touches life line

These people are very easily hurt in relationships. It can take them many years to get over a break-up, that's if they ever do at all. I have found this line on very sensitive people who lack self-confidence and at times need reassurance about themselves. Carriers of this line were never really encouraged or felt valued as children by their parents growing up, especially if it is found on the non-dominant or passive hand.

Loving and sympathetic are their strong points, especially when it comes to matters of the heart. They are a great shoulder to cry

Major lines

Heart line dropping to life line

on because they understand the pain of hurt and love. I have seen many great counsellors who have this heart line. They can become quite emotionally insecure at times, due to not feeling good about themselves. This is where jealousy raises it head. But by putting themselves out there at parties, work functions and meeting new people, they will build their self-confidence and worth.

Flirt

If there are many little lines at the end of the heart line, this person likes to flirt and enjoys the thrill of having many connections with many different people. They can also find themselves in unconventional relationships, due to them enjoying diversity, spontaneity when it comes to matters of the heart.

Double heart line

These are quite rare, but I have witnessed a few people who were very kind, loving and sensitive people. They're very loyal and generous to those that are close to them. They can be very intuitive and sensitive to the environment they find themselves in. They can sense the tension in the air as well as the love and happiness. The double

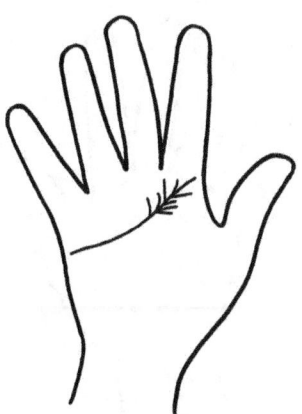

Heart flirt lines

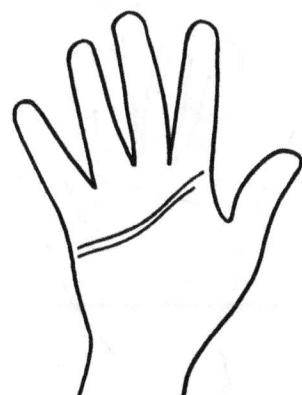

Double heart line

71

heart line also offers protection against upsets and disappointments in all matters of love and romance. They also enjoy a couple of passions at the same time, which means a lot to them.

A line from the heart line touching the head line

When the heart line drops to the head line, there's emotional and mental confusion in your life at that particular time. Maybe you were being controlled by a more dominant or possessive partner, and saw a different side of your partner that you didn't know existed. These lines when seen on your hand are quite significant as they show you a different reality to those that you live aren't perfect and have flaws.

A line from the heart line touching the head line. A time of much emotional and mental confusion.

A small rise on the heart line under the ring/Apollo finger

When the heart line rises under the ring/Apollo finger, these people are attracted to people who are gifted in these traits, and are obviously creatives such as actors, musicians and painters. They are a little bit left of centre, and attractive to the opposite sex and charismatic. They make fun and adventurous partners.

Rise underneath Apollo

Rise underneath Saturn

A small rise on the heart line under the middle/Saturn finger

When the heart line rises under the middle/Saturn finger. These people are attracted to the qualities of the Saturnarian traits, such as duty and responsibility, people of authority and they take life seriously. They go into the army, police officers, government officials and anyone else who upholds the law, like a lawyer.

Heart line dipping under Mercury

A small dip of the heart line under the little/Mercury finger

When this is seen, the person will dislike business or any type of venture that is based on greed. They enjoy an alternative lifestyle, they believe in peace and harmony and taking care of planet Earth. I have found this on many alternative, natural therapists, such as homeopaths, nutritionists, chiropractors and the like.

Heart line dipping under Saturn

When the heart line dips under the middle/Saturn finger

When there is a dip under the middle/Saturn finger, these people are emotionally disgruntled by a partner who had no regard for their feelings and treated them terribly. If a young female under the age of twenty-one is wearing a ring on this finger, it's a dead giveaway that they are trying to let go of anger and frustration of an ex-boyfriend. Usually a dip under the middle/Saturn finger can also mean anger and resentment toward a father who was never around or didn't care for their child. Because of this, they go on to dislike anyone of authority or in the government. They don't like being told what to do and become very independent and self-sufficient.

A floating heart line

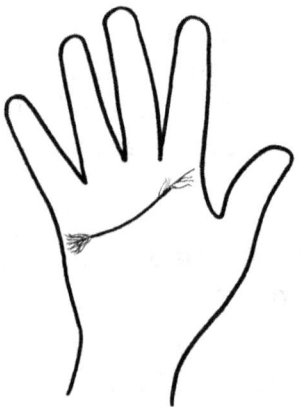

Lines running up and down the heart line, as well as the feathered appearance under Mercury.

Floating heart line

When the heart line doesn't attach or begin at percussion (the side of the palm), these people are connected to animals and nature, but not other people. They prefer the company of and prefer to work with animals, long walks in the forest or be by themselves. I read for a lady once who had never had a boyfriend, an she preferred her own company and had a dog grooming business. This lady had a floating heart line.

Lines running off the heart line

Upwards

Lines running upwards signify happy events, emotional highs, a positive outlook at this time.

Downwards

Lines running downward from the heart line signify negative upsetting events, upsets in relationships, misfortune and sorrow at the time the lines can be seen.

Feathered

At the beginning of the heart line, just under the little /Mercury finger, if the line has a feathered look, this person was brought up in a home with a lot of tension and quarrelling. The environment was unpleasant for this person, usually the parents got divorced when the child was old enough to understand what was going on between their parents. If seen on both passive and dominant hands, this earlier period of tension has been brought into the future, and will be an underlying issue in their relationships or when parenting.

CURVED HEART LINE

So, remember curved heart lines have a more dominant, masculine, physical approach to love, where a straight heart line has a more passive, feminine attitude.

Short heart lines

Have not experienced as many different emotions or feelings, as someone with a long heart line. Short heart line people aren't as outgoing or open as their longer counterparts.
- When the line is curved, there's warmth and demonstration.
- When the line is straight, there's thoughtfulness and consideration.
- When the line is short they are sexually motivated with no attachment.

Will my romance last the distance?

The quickest and easiest way to know if your partnership, marriage, friendship will last the distance, is to check to see if the heart lines are similar. If they are, then that's good news, because you'll understand each other in matters of feelings, love and sex.

If they are different, you'll both have to make it work, with much more love and understanding, due to the emotional needs being different from each other. Make sure you both know each others' strengths and weaknesses when it comes to matters of the heart. This is so you will be in a better position to deal with love's windy path. It is better to be forewarned than forearmed.

HOW DEEP IS THE LINE

Deep

When the line is deep, like it is cut into the palm, this person is very emotional and will always listen to what the heart tells them. They'll change their attitude depending on what they are feeling which can alter at any given moment, depending on their mood.

Deep red

These people express their feelings and emotions very deeply. They can have a great display of laughter or sadness with great intensity. Due to using up a lot of high emotional energy, there could be a heart problem or high blood pressure.

Faint

People with faint lines don't know how to express their feelings and can withdraw into themselves, feeling overwhelmed at times. They may at times come across cold and distant with little emphasis put on emotional fulfilment in their lives. At times they suffer from low energy levels.

Strong and clean

If the heart line is strong and clear, these people are generous, open with plenty of warmth and love to give. There are no emotional hang-ups about love or relationships.

MARKINGS ON THE HEART LINE

Islands

Islands on the heart line can denote depression, emotional confusion and heart troubles. Sometimes, in matters of love, we want it but fear rejection and this is when an island will show up.

If there's an island under the ring or Apollo finger, there will be eyesight difficulties. I had a client today who said she was off to the optometrist because she couldn't see. Sure enough, there was an island under the ring/Apollo finger on the heart line.

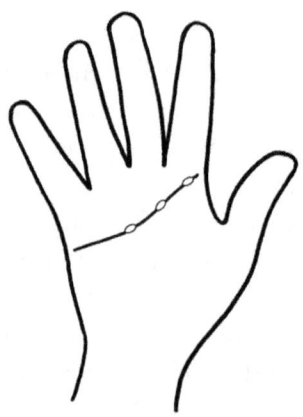
Heart line with many islands

A break

When there is a break on the heart line, this can mean a rejection, divorce, split or death of a loved one, which really affected you. A line starting above the break and running parallel is a fortunate sign. Means a positive outcome and you'll move on with someone else. If there is a line below the break, it will take some time for the wound to heal, but you will eventually move on emotionally.

Broken heart line

Major lines

A deeply cut heart line

A circle

When there is a circle on the heart line, this can mean a physical problem with your heart, such as heart disease, palpitations, murmurs.

Lines intercepting

Vertical lines going through the heart line are disturbances from people, Challenges, life difficulties, which have hurt or upset you. It is also a display of how easily the person may be affected by life in general. If there are many lines, the person is sensitive and feels a lot more and their disposition would be more fragile. Someone who has fewer intercepting lines usually rolls with the punches and moves on in life, not letting these disturbances affect them.

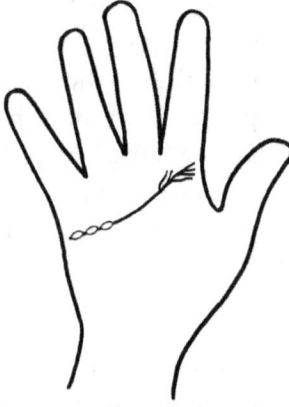
Heart line displaying circles and lines

POSITIONING OF THE HEART LINE

Close to head line

When the heart line is close to the head line, the heart rules the head.

Close to fingers

When the heart line is high up close to the bottom of the fingers, the head rules the heart.

Balance of space

If there is a good balance of space between the heart and head lines, the person will listen to their reason and intuition before making a decision. They are very level headed.

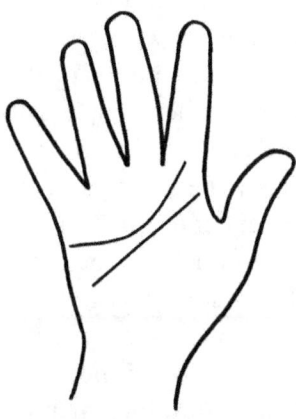
Narrow space between heart and head lines

Heart line close to fingers

Large space between heart and head lines

Heart and head lines fused into one line, referred to as the Simian line

Too much space

If there is too much space between the two lines, the person will be very open minded, an original thinker, who is an individual and doesn't follow the herd. They enjoy their freedom, and are always independent of the good thoughts of everybody else.

No space

People with no space in between the heart and head lines are closed minded, and they like to look at their feelings, always asking questions to see if they've said or done the right thing, when dealing with other people. At times, they can be very critical of themselves, paranoid and judgemental when it comes to dealing with affections of the heart and their loved ones.

Joined together

When the heart line and the head lines are fused into one, this is called the Simian line. These people get their thoughts and feelings confused and become irritated. There's a lot of inner tension, as they can have a lot of difficulty in relating to other people. Most of the time, there can be outbursts of anger or sadness depending on what's going on at any given moment. There's usually inner tension and not a feeling of ease. Meditation or yoga is brilliant for these people, as it calms the thoughts to this person. Inner peace and stillness is a by-product of meditation, and is the perfect remedy. The

Major lines

Simian lined hand is always focussed, strong willed and most of the time, achieves great things in life because they're so determined. But they need an off switch, as they tend to burn the candle at both ends, which is to their detriment.

QUIZ TIME QUESTIONS

1. If a person has a long heart line, are they open and loving with lots of friendships?
2. If you have a curved heart line, is sexual expression important to you?
3. If you have a straight heart line, would you be a passive or dominant partner?
4. If you are really choosy and an idealist when it comes to relationships, where would your heart line end?
5. If sex plays an important role in your life and you don't like emotional attachments, where would your heart line end?
6. If you have an island under the ring or Apollo finger, what problem would you have?
7. If the heart line is deeply cut with the colour of red, would you say the person has no enthusiasm or vitality when it comes to matters of the heart?
8. If there is a Simian line present, would you be open and relaxed?
9. What's the most fortunate heart line to have?
10. If you have a spray of small lines at the end of your heart line, what would this mean?

Answers

1. Yes, they enjoy many types of friendships and connections. **2.** Yes, sex is very important and they like to be demonstrative and expressive when it comes to relationships. **3.** You would be the passive partner because you are more thoughtful and caring. **4.** The heart line would end under the index or Jupiter finger. **5.** The heart line will end with a curve under the middle or Saturn finger. **6.** You'll have an eyesight problem. **7.** No, they would have an abundance of enthusiasm and vitality, and are highly emotional and can be very passionate with their partners. **8.** No, they can come across a little distant with a lot of inner tension if they don't have avenues to clear their thoughts and feelings. **9.** Three branches at the end of the heart line. These people require emotional, mental and physical stimulation. They like to get the best out of life and others. **10.** You are flirtatious and enjoy many different connections with people.

THE HEAD LINE

How do you like to think? Are you rational with your thoughts? Do you like to think well into the future or do you like to think short term? Are you practical and level headed or do you like to use your imagination and intuition, thinking and living life in a mystical, subjective way? The head line is all about how you think, but not how smart you are.

A strong, deep head line which is straight, finishing underneath Apollo. This length is considered average

Strong head line

If the head line is strong and clear with no breaks and reaches out underneath the ring or Apollo finger, which is considered average, you think rationally and logically. With the ability to come to your own conclusions, on your own without the help of others. You definitely have a good head on your shoulders without being persuaded by peers, and are an independent thinker.

When the head line is the strongest on the hand, you'll like to use your energy thinking. Focus, awareness and attention to detail are common traits of a deep, strong head line.

How long is the line?

Anywhere past the ring or Apollo finger is considered long and reaching onto the little or Mercury finger. These people like to think about things well into the future. I have seen this line on people who are consultants of any kind. They like to go into every kind of detail and consider everything before making decisions. They like to learn and read a lot and know a lot about everything. They enjoy titbits of information and facts. These people are great at Cluedo or Trivial Pursuit, and always check headlines of your opponents in

Major lines

A long, clear, straight head line, ending under Mercury

order to get on the right team, otherwise you are a goner. Entrepreneurs and business owners who like to do things their own way, have this head line. A downside to the head line ending under the little or Mercury finger, is over analysing and making the mind go into overdrive, and this can cause these people a lot of stress. They enjoy introspection about their lives and what's going on, but when it is overdone, as seen in the long head line, it can stop their lives, quite literally, until they put themselves back into the moment. Albert Einstein possessed a long straight head line.

Does it go too far?

A head line reaching to the other side

When the line reaches to the other side of the hand, this person is constantly thinking, and they never switch off, and their thinking is very detailed and comprehensive. I have seen this line on accountants, and anybody working with numbers and formulas have this head line. At times the person with this head line enjoys their own space and can be seen as quite cold emotionally, cutting themselves off from those close to them. They have great focus and are able to switch off to what's going on around them. Great insight and intelligence is a positive factor, but at times if the balance in their lives isn't right, with emotional intelligence, family, friends and colleagues, they can be left out in the cold. I once had a regular client who possessed this line and each time I saw him, he had published another book, five to his credit. He was a well-known psychologist who lectured around the world, and still is the best in his field. However, because he was too interested in his intellectual life and not his family, they all didn't want to know him, until he started working on getting back the connections he once had with them.

Short head line underneath Saturn

Now the short of it

People who have short head lines are practical and straight to the point. They like to focus on one thing at a time and always have a unique ability in one area of their lives. There is no imagination here, nothing lies beneath the surface, and thinking things through isn't on their radar. They go by impulse and do what has to be done now, the future doesn't exist to these people. How short is short? When the head line ends underneath the middle or Saturn finger. Whatever is happening now is what they think about, nothing more, nothing less.

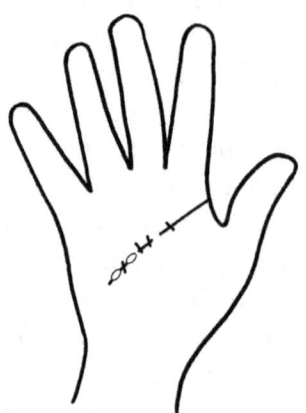

A head line with breaks, islands and influence lines

Scattered minds

When the head line has breaks, islands or little vertical lines going through the line, this person will be scattered, and have an inability to focus and concentrate with times of depression and mental anguish. They're easily distracted by what's going on around them, or what happened to them in the past. Relaxation techniques like meditation and yoga should be used to calm the mind and soothe their spirits. This will give them a sense of peace within and give them the ability to focus on one thing at a time, and let them enjoy life one moment at a time.

Is it straight or does it curve?

There are two forms of a head line, straight or a curve. These people who have either one live in separate worlds from one another and view it differently.

Major lines

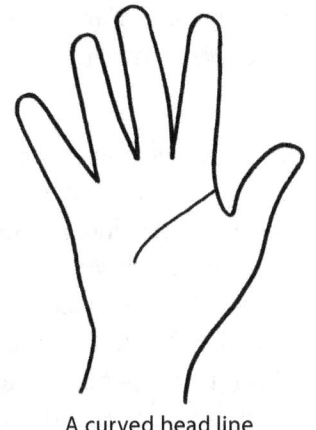

A curved head line

Curved

Curved head line people are imaginative and like to play around with ideas and insights. They enjoy thinking in different ways, and there is never just one way to draw a conclusion or make a decision. It's all about perspective and interpretation. There are always two sides to a coin, nothing is as simple and as straightforward as we think. The way they think depends on how they feel, the environment they are in, the weather, and who is around them. These people enjoy the arts, museums, plays, theatre, poetry and anything else that takes them away from the mundane and into the mystical world which they enjoy.

Curved head line people like to be on their own at times, so that they can reach for meaning in what's happening in their lives. They've got a tendency to withdraw from this world and go somewhere else into their imaginations. They can be seen as loners and enjoy their need for self-reflection, which is very important and beneficial for them.

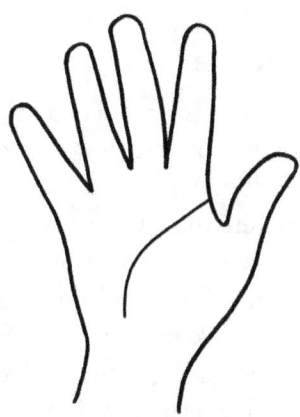

A deeply curved head line, reaching onto the Mount of Luna

Deeply curved

When the head line curves deeply onto the Mount of Luna, the qualities of a curved head line are at the extreme. They can, at times, live in a world of fantasy and find it difficult to operate in the real world. They're extremely sensitive and need some way to channel and express pent up energy as they can be very creative and artistic. If they don't express themselves in some form, melancholy and depression will settle in. I have found that many very successful artists, poets, fiction writers and spiritually gifted psychics and healers, have these deeply curved head lines. People who carry this head line also have very vivid dreams with lots of colour, and unusual places, that stir up their emotions. These dreams can be recalled and felt for a very long time, even years after.

A straight, long head line

If it is straight

The straight head line person is very straightforward, practical and likes to go from A to B with nothing in the middle. They're analytical, rational and logical and they are not interested in emotions, only the details and the cold, hard facts. I've found that people who are good with adding numbers in their heads have a straight head line. Many good business executives, accountants, scientists all have this line.

WHERE DOES THE HEAD LINE BEGIN

The beginning of the head line starts under the index or Jupiter finger, in four possible variations. The position of the head line tells you how confident, self-sufficient, and open minded someone is, or how dependent, close minded or controlled they were by parents before the age of twenty-one.

Head line not attached to life line

Head line off life line

When the head line is not tied to the life line, this person is independent of thought and action. They're self-sufficient due to when they were younger, one or two parents weren't around for them, or a lot of responsibility was placed on them to look after their brothers and sisters. They brought themselves up and with this they learnt to think for themselves and become self-sufficient and get the job done.

People with a spacing around one centimetre can be seen as impulsive, unconventional, and who like to give things a go and take risks. Usually, they've got their own businesses or are leaders in companies.

They're open minded and like to experience life with everything it has to offer.

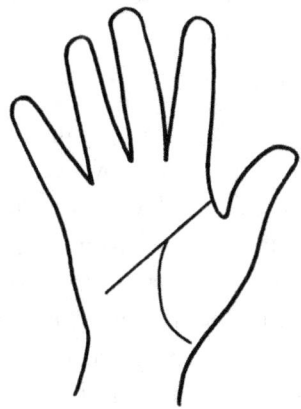
Head line tied to the life line

Head line attached

When the head line is tied to the life line, this person was under the control of their parents up until the head line leaves the life line. They've been in the same house in which they grew up in and followed rules and regulations that their parents set out for them. Because of their parents' actions, they're not as confident or self-sufficient as they should be for their age. They really don't like to think for themselves, and they're really cautious and second opinions are always valued.

Beginning on the mount of jupiter

These people are go-getters, very ambitious and highly independent. They're really open-minded who will take on life with all they have to get the results that they want. This head line beginning is a very favourable sign as all the people that I've read for have all done extremely well in their chosen fields. My little niece, Peri, has this marking and I look forward to seeing her do very well in her life if she applies herself.

Head line beginning on the Mount of Jupiter

Head line beginning within the life line

This person is very uncertain about themselves and the place that they keep in the world. They're shy and insecure and are very sensitive, and they keep to the tried and the tested as the safest bet to play. They look for and need people around them to give them the help and confidence they require to move forward, giving them the surety they need. By getting out of their safe zones and stepping outside into

Head line beginning inside the life line

the unknown, is the quickest way for them to grow, mature and evolve, slow and steady always wins the race, and a motto they should live by.

Point to remember

Always look at both of your palms to gain further insight into how you've grown and matured, and what's stayed the same on the palm of your hands. For instance, if on the passive hand, the head line is tied to the life line, the person was under their parents' control or rule, but as they left that environment they took risks and started becoming independent and self-sufficient.

The right hand or dominant hand will show after the age of twenty-one, that the head line is no longer tied to the life line, but a gap has appeared, thus showing independence of thought, confidence, ambition and someone who likes to stand on their own two feet, which they have done.

When looking at your palms, it's not the obvious and normal that will intrigue and fascinate you. But what has changed on your palms, that's where you're learning that you have changed your life, by your actions and what you do every moment of every day. So, don't waste time, it's the most valuable commodity that we have, once it is gone, it can never be turned back.

A head line with a large fork

Fork

At the end of the head line, if you see a large fork, this is where there has been a split or change in a way a person thinks. When it's straight at the beginning, the thought is logical and rational, but an experience or an event changed the mindset where something didn't add up. So, you started to use your imagination, creativity and intuition to seek the answers to life's challenges.

Small fork

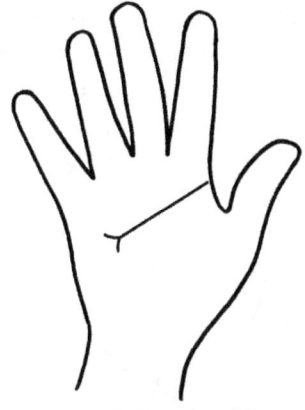

Writers' fork on head line

When there's a small fork at the end of the head line, this is called the Writers' Fork. Don't assume straight away just because this is present, but look to the little or Mercury finger, and look to see if it's longer than average. If not, you'll be able to express yourself with the written word, either through novels, non-fiction or poetry. Also if you do have a fork at the end of your head line, you'll have the ability to see two sides of a story. I have seen this on the hands of judges, lawyers and journalists, and with this is usually accompanied with a head line separate to the life line. These people know there are always two sides to a story.

Line rising to the Mount of Mercury

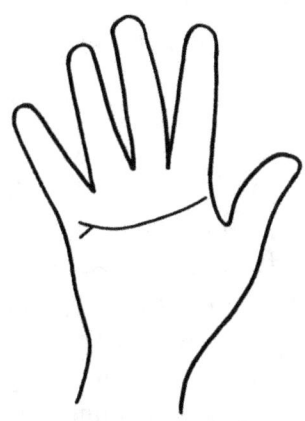

Head line rising to the Mount of Mercury

When there's a small line that rises at the end of the head line towards the Mount of Mercury, this person is someone who is good at making money through ideas, they like to invent to make quick dollars. People who have this little line usually work for themselves.

Breaks

When the head line breaks and it can happen anywhere along the line, this is a stage in your life when you started to see things differently, usually due to a head trauma, severe shock, a loss of a loved one, or a job giving you stress, or a breakdown. Most of the time the line will take on a different direction. So, if it was straight, then slopes down, or if it curved down at the beginning, but becomes straight after the break.

Islands

Whenever you see an island on the head line, there's mental confusion, sensitivity to stress in your life. Most of the time, transitions of the life cycle are occurring, such as stepping out into the unknown, a new job, moving overseas, an island will appear at that time. From my own experiences, meditation or enjoying a hobby that makes you lose track of time, will create inner peace to bring back stability when it is needed the most. So, you can regain mental clarity and focus.

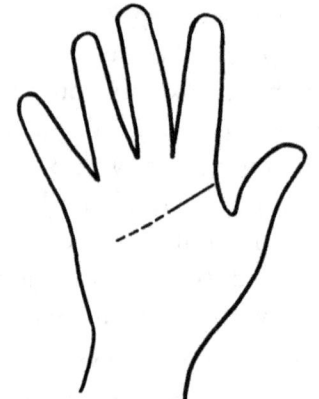
A head line with many breaks

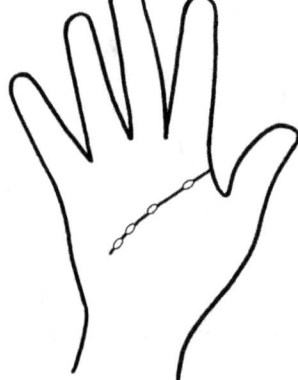
Islands on the head line

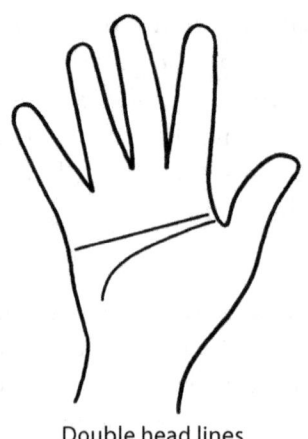
Double head lines

Double head lines

Yes, you better believe it. I have seen this on a few bright characters who have the ability to think and act differently, around different people and situations. Most of the time, these people are working professionals who have highly paid, successful careers, but can change the way they think and act around loved ones when they are not in the workplace arena.

HEAD LINE THAT RUNS CLOSE TO THE LIFE LINE

The head line that runs close to the life line is a sign of a mystic, a person who believes in synchronicity, signs, messages and divine intervention. They're very spiritual and sensitive who find it hard to operate in this world. Often they believe and say they don't belong

Major lines

Head line that runs close to the life line

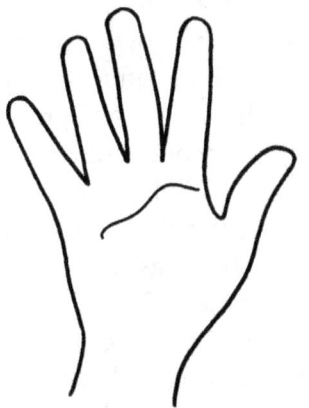

Wavy head line

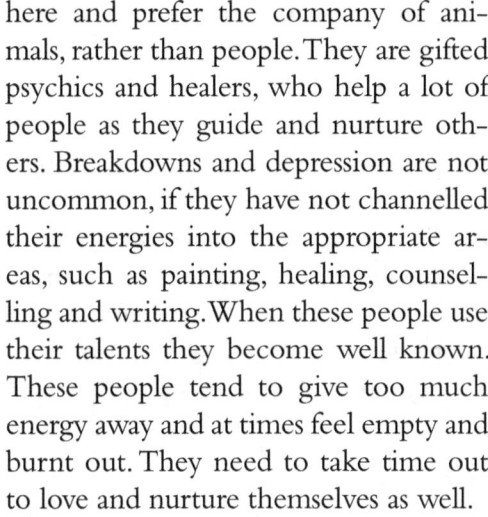

here and prefer the company of animals, rather than people. They are gifted psychics and healers, who help a lot of people as they guide and nurture others. Breakdowns and depression are not uncommon, if they have not channelled their energies into the appropriate areas, such as painting, healing, counselling and writing. When these people use their talents they become well known. These people tend to give too much energy away and at times feel empty and burnt out. They need to take time out to love and nurture themselves as well.

Wavy

These people like to think for themselves and like to come up with their own original ideas and concepts. They're always coming from a different angle and enjoy thinking outside the box. Even more so if the head line sits on the Mount of Jupiter at the beginning of the head line.

QUIZ TIME QUESTIONS

1. What's considered long, when it comes to the head line?
2. When the head lines goes all the way to the other side of the palm, do these people get totally absorbed in their own lives and neglect those around them?
3. If you have a short head line, would you have many interests and hobbies on the go at the same time?
4. Does a person who has many breaks in the head line have the ability to think clearly and focus on the present moment?
5. Is a curved head line person more likely to think practically and

logically, or use their imagination and creativity?
6. When the head line is detached from the life line would this person in their life, play it safe and not take any risks?
7. If the head line is attached to the life line of a person, would the parents be a major influence in this person's life before the age of twenty-one?
8. When the head line begins well inside the life line, would you say the person is confident and ambitious?
9. When a person has a break on the head line, what has happened to them?
10. Would you say a person with islands on the head line could deal with stress and confusion effectively?

Answers:

1. Anywhere past the ring or Apollo finger is considered long. **2.** Yes, they focus their minds and absorb themselves in their own lives, can be seen as self-centred, shutting everyone and outside influences out. **3.** No, these people like to do one thing at a time, enjoy the present moment and have a unique skill. **4.** No, these people are stressed, scattered and confused due to a deep upset or loss which has made them feel vulnerable. **5.** Imagination and creativity rule the day here. **6.** No, they like to take risks, are independent, ambitious and at times, impatient. **7.** Yes, they have been under their parents' influence and rule. **8.** No, they would feel insecure, needy and always looking for reassurances from those around them. **9.** Mental stress or breakdown has occurred through loss or hardship. **10.** No, these people are sensitive to stress.

LIFE LINE

Will I die young or will I live to a very ripe, old age? These are the two main questions being fired at me. When it comes to looking at the life line, if I was a gypsy fortune teller from times gone by, I would tell you what you wanted to hear, depending on how much silver you were prepared to give me. The more I get, the longer you'll live and the greater your fortune.

Unfortunately, those days are long gone, and this line has nothing to do with how long you live. It deals with how strong your constitution is for living. Zest, vitality and enthusiasm with the love of life can be seen here, and how much you like to give out to those around you. Do you like to focus on achieving your vision, making life interesting and fun, or do you like to stay in one place, to stay with the known, predictable and comfortable, enjoying the illusion of stability and security?

The long and short of it

A long life line

Long

When the line is long and deep without any breaks or islands and has a nice wide arc out into the middle of the palm, this person has good health and energy in abundance and likes to take on life's challenges. They've got a strong, healthy constitution, never seeing the inside of a medical centre. They enjoy healthy relationships with family and friends, and are quite positive in life. When an upset or illness does occur, they've got great coping skills and it doesn't take them too long to get better. Psychologically, they move on pretty quickly from their woes and disappointments and are ready to embrace the sunshine again. With a positive attitude, they endure all of what life throws at them and adapt well to change. They have their feet planted firmly on the ground with reality and life, they can be an inspirational influence to others.

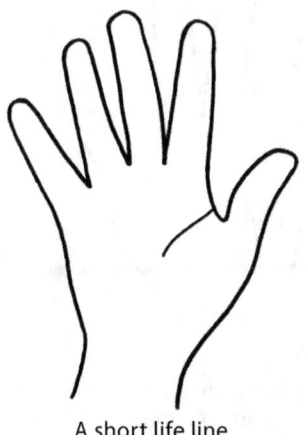

A short life line

Short

People with short life lines that are deep without any breaks or islands, have energy for the moment, but not for the remaining years ahead. If they introduce a good healthy eating and exercise plan, and a hobby, this will reduce stress and create the spark of initiative back into their lives. The more meaning and purpose we strive for, a much better chance we have of creating happiness and vitality within our lives. By building on a stronger constitution, this gives the short life line person a brighter outlook and a bountiful and enjoyable future.

Normal or common life line

Normal position

Usually there can be a few common endings with the life line. The most common is around the Mount of Venus, which is underneath the thumb. This person likes to enjoy the creature comforts of their home. They usually stick to what's convenient, comfortable and familiar to them. Travelling is always within their own country and not too far away from their home.

Ending in a fork

When the life line ends in a fork, which is seen on both of my hands, this person likes to travel abroad and seek out exotic and exciting places. Where the fork begins on the life line is when the person starts to get itchy feet, becoming restless and in life to some extent. I have found that people who have the fork love to travel and like to enjoy other cultures and experience a different way of life. Most of the people with the fork that I have read for move to another country to live or are just avid travellers, especially if the life line ends on the Mount of Luna. The majority of people who do travel for a living,

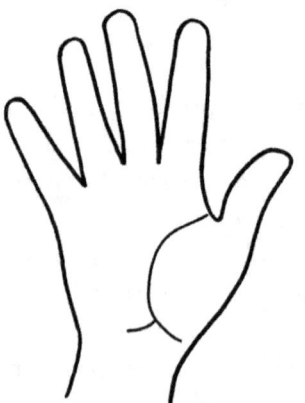

Life line with fork

Life line ending on the Mount of Luna

such as pilots, air hostesses, world class athletes, all have this fork to a varying degree.

I have read in books and had discussions surrounding where the fork has its beginning on the life line, that this person starts to lose energy, feel drained and lethargic. I don't believe this to be true. But the person with the fork has travelled a long way in their life, away from their family roots and achieved a lot more than their parents did and where they grew up.

Breaks

Breaks along the life line are caused by many things that cause us to lose our strength, energy and vitality. A sudden break up, loss of a loved one, unemployment and illness, can all make the life line split and create conflict in our lives.

When the line breaks up and there's an overlap with a sister line on the outside of the life line, this is a fortunate sign. This means life will get better for you, due to circumstances improving, getting you out of your comfort zone, being challenged, learning from your mistakes and becoming more self-reliant.

For instance, I have a friend who was divorced at the age of thirty-five, so there was a break in his life line, but shortly after there was an overlapping life line recommencing. To this day, life is much better for him with a more compatible partner, an enjoyable lifestyle that suits them both and he has had a promotion at work.

No overlap

But, if the life line breaks with no overlaps, there will be a delay in your life, putting your life on hold, sometimes for a few years, while you get over an illness, mental turmoil, or unemployment. Life will get better, but it will take time.

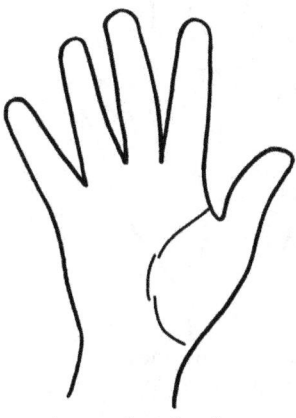

An overlapping line after a break

Break on passive hand

If you have a break on your passive hand before the age of twenty-one, this could be from a loss of a parent, parents divorcing, serious illness, or your parents and yourself moved around a lot when you were younger.

Now check your active dominant hand, and where there are no breaks, you have created a lifestyle and living which is much more stable, healthier and positive to your needs.

Rising lines

When there are small lines rising from the life line, I have found these to be a positive influence, and events which make you happy and are memorable like the birth of a child, getting married, travelling or a job promotion. They're like sparks of vitality that make you enjoy and embrace life at the time they are found.

Descending lines

These little lines descend from the life line, causing you to lose energy and vitality. They're seen as negative experiences, like the loss of a job or a friendship, feeling disillusioned with your life, a loss of a house, or motor vehicle. Whatever the loss is, it's of value to you and it dampens your spirits for a short period of time.

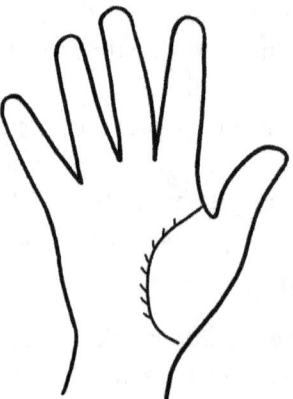

Rising lines on the life line

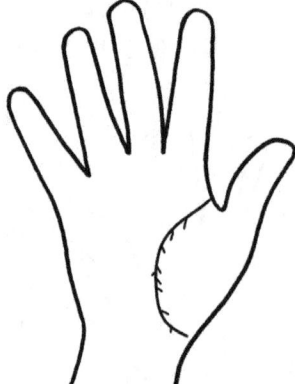

Descending lines from the life line

Islands

Islands can be seen as times of stress, confusion or illness. When an island appears, I have often found it's due to unhappiness within the home or work place. Islands can be seen as a negative and a delay of vitalilty and enthusiasm, at the time they appear.

Bar lines

When you see little lines going through the life line, they can be seen as interruptions from outside your control, circumstances that occur to you which you didn't see coming. They usually come from family or friends that stop you from moving on at the time. These interruptions are only temporary, and can be seen from the family ring. A ring is a vertical line at the base of the thumb, and will be discussed in Chapter 11, Bars, Marking and Signs.

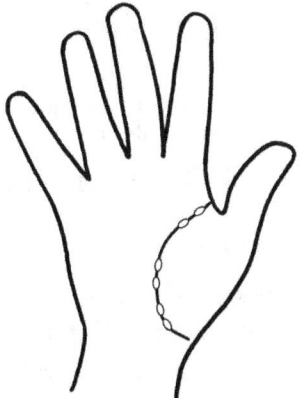
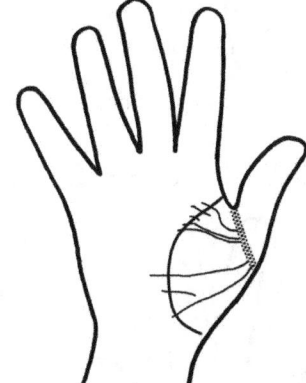

Islands on the life line

Bar lines go through the life line. Family ring is near the thumb. Influence lines coming from the family ring.

Two life lines

This is very rare, but I've seen a couple of people who have two life lines, and it is unique when spotted. This person is living a double life, married to two people in different states or countries, two homes and different identities.

Also it may show a family man in one country, and a bachelor in another. It might be a good time for you ladies to check your partner's hand just for laughs. It may also indicate a person who divides their time in different countries with two homes, enjoying the culture's food and activities as well.

Feathering

This can be seen at the start of the life line, denoting a stressful situation within the home, a sensitive child who was put under a lot of strain, due to their parents fighting and arguing, or a divorce, or a major illness that the child had before the age of twenty-one.

Two life lines

Feathering at the beginning of the life line

HOW FAR IS THE CURVE OF THE LIFE LINE

Wide, curving life line

Nice wide curve

When there's a nice curve reaching out to the middle of the palm, this person will enjoy change and travel, have a good social network and have plenty of energy to do what they like to do without too many restrictions. They have an abundance of energy to set goals and see them through to completion. They like to listen to their instincts and take life on with full force.

Clinging to thumb

Life line clings to thumb

When the line clings to the thumb and is only slightly curved, this person likes family life, and doesn't like to venture out from this familiar space too often. People with this life line can be seen as introverted, shy and likes to enjoy their own company. They don't like change or travel, but sticking to the familiar. They can lack warmth, vitality and can be seen as reserved, especially when there is no Venus Mount, and the base of the thumb is flat, without any rise.

Thick, healthy life line

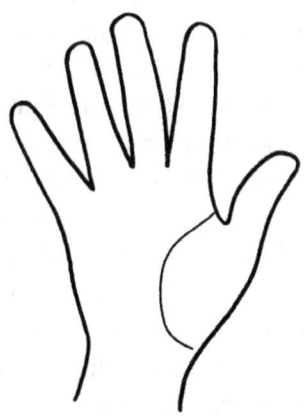

Thin life line

Thick life line

When you see that your life line is thicker than your other major lines, this denotes that you've got a strong constitution, plenty of strength, stamina and vitality. You are always on the go, enjoying life, travel and change, and are hardly ever ill. If you do get sick, you bounce back rather quickly, due to your positive outlook on life.

Thin life line

If you have a thin life line, that lacks thickness and colour, physical vitality and enthusiasm won't be your strong suit. You may lack the energy to get through the day, feeling drained by life and people. Ill health tends to plague you due to poor eating and sleeping habits. I have seen, in time, with a better healthy living regimen, exercising, sleeping eight hours a night and a good selection of nutritious foods, this line becomes thicker with a healthier pink, red colour.

QUIZ TIME QUESTIONS

1. If the life line is long, without any breaks or islands, and has a wide curve, will the person be sick with no energy or vitality to get through their life?
2. When the life line is short, does this mean that you'll have a short life?
3. Do people with a fork at the end of their life line dislike travel and change?
4. If there is a break in the life line, does that disrupt our energy and

vitality for short periods of time?
5. Is having two life lines rare?
6. When an island appears on the life line, does that denote health and strength?
7. Is an overlap after a break a fortunate sign to see?
8. Are rising lines on the life line a fortunate sign, and what do they mean?
9. Does feathering at the beginning of the life line mean that you had a happy, healthy childhood?
10. Bar lines going through the life line are they fortunate signs or interruptions from outside influencers, which were out of your control?

Answers:

1. No, these people have a strong constitution and are rarely sick, they have vast amounts of energy and zest and have an enthusiastic approach to life. **2.** No, it means that they've got energy and vitality for the now. **3.** No, these people have a restless nature and enjoy travelling or may travel for work. **4.** Yes, the energy and health we once had, stops for a short period of time, due to minor setbacks and unforeseen circumstances. **5.** Yes, it's very rare and unique. **6.** No, islands appear due to times of stress, confusion and illness. **7.** Yes, it's a fortunate sign as things always work out for the better, a more rewarding job, a more fulfilling relationship, better health and lifestyle. **8.** Yes, they represent good moments in your life, such as the birth of a child, inheritance, a new job or a new home. **9.** No, there was disharmony in the home, a lot of fighting, arguing, a divorce, neglected children or a serious illness at this time in their life. **10.** They're unfortunate signs from outside influences, usually from family that were out of your control.

EIGHT

Minor Lines

Study yourself; it should be the best subject you learn and the one you revise each and every day. — *EVAN SUTTER*

FATE LINE

Although this line is called the fate line, it has nothing to do with fate. It has to do with your career path of stability and security. The fate line can give you information such as, Are you going to dedicate your career to just one path or many? Will you work with the public, or be self-employed? Do you work in the family business or enjoy having a couple of jobs at one time?

Usually difficult to locate, but not that hard to find, it's a vertical line that can be traced down underneath the middle/Saturn finger, heading towards the wrist. Sometimes it ends under the middle/Saturn finger, but it can end under any of your fingers, depending on what type of work that you do.

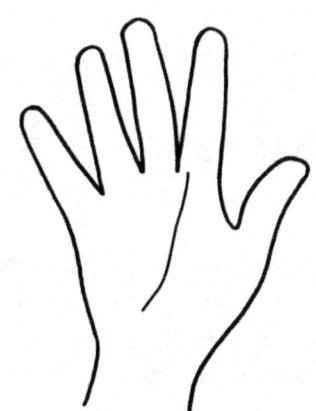

Fate line ending under Jupiter

Ending under index/Jupiter finger

The person that has the fate line ending under the index/Jupiter finger, usually works for themselves in a small business or their own company. Most of the time, they're very entrepreneurial, always striving to use all of their talents and abilities, utilising their potential. They are ambitious leaders who think outside the box. I've seen this line ending under the index/Jupiter finger on many specialists and successful business owners.

Ending under middle/Saturn finger

These people usually work for large organisations and companies, most of the time government or private enterprise. They like the emphasis of duty and responsibility, with the rules and regulations that have to be adhered to and followed. These people never stray from outside the line.

Ending under ring/Apollo finger

These people are the creatives in life. They are artistic and love to use their imaginations to create beauty in the world, with all of its joy and splendour. They can be musicians, novelists, actors, painters, anyone who brings depth and substance into our society, giving it colour and depth.

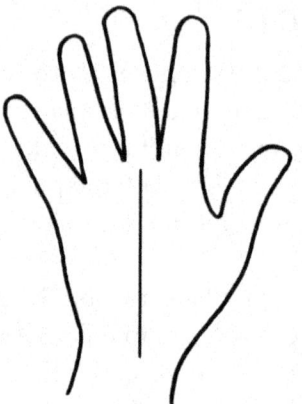
Fate line ending under Saturn

Fate line ending under Apollo

Don't be upset or frazzled if you don't have one, most people don't, and if we do, it can be faint, scratchy or deeply etched, which gives it prominent placing within the hand.

WHERE DOES THE FATE LINE COMMENCE?

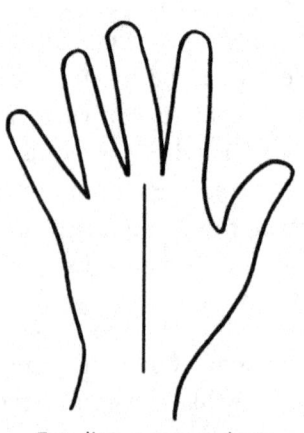
Fate line commencing in the middle

In the middle

Down the bottom of the wrist, this person knew what they wanted to do, when they were really young. They followed the necessary steps to get where they wanted to go, so from school onwards, they did the appropriate subjects and achieved the grades to get into university. They went for the interview to get the work experience they required to get the position. Once there, they usually diversify within the place of work until their retirement. This fate line, nine times out of ten, finishes under the middle/Saturn finger.

This would be considered a long straight fate line, dedicated to the one path throughout their working life. I've seen this line on people who have stayed in the same career for forty years plus, and they believe that working in this job was their destiny and gave them true satisfaction.

My brother David has this fate line, he wanted to be a policeman since he was a little boy, and to this very day he enjoys serving the community in which he lives.

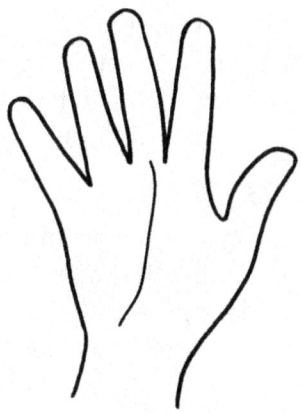

Fate line commencing on Luna

On the Mount of Luna

If your line commences on the Mount of Luna, these people will deal with the public and use their outgoing personality to a great extent. People who are quite creative have their fate lines beginning here. They are free spirits, and enjoy change and travel. They don't like to be tied down to conformity and enjoy the spiritual side to life. These people have gone against what their parents wanted for them, as they believe living for what you want to be is very important – and it is!

On or within the life line

If your fate line is found on or within the life line, you'll work in the family business, or work in a profession that your parents wanted you to do. Most of the time when you have obstacles and challenges in your life, you refer to your parents and family to help with the decisions about what is going on.

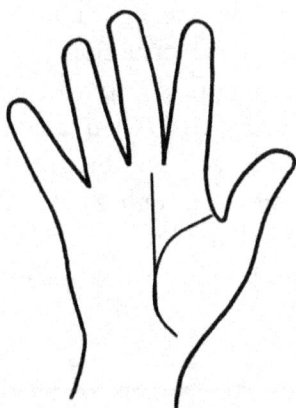

Fate line attached to life line

Absent

When the line is absent from the palm, it just means you've followed your own path, wherever that may lead. These people haven't fallen in with the status quo or given into their parent's wishes, rather, they have gone their own sweet way. This gives them a feeling of freedom and a taste of many different jobs. Some of the people that I've read for have gone onto be successful, self-made millionaires.

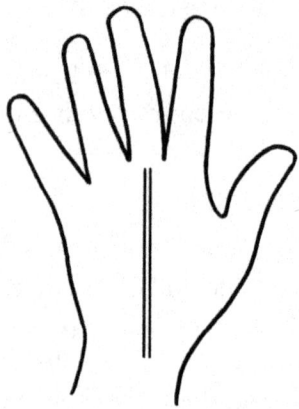

Two fate lines side by side

Parallel lines

Sometimes we have two jobs or two different career paths at the same time, this is the meaning of the two parallel lines side by side. Men and women looking after children, then going to work full time, a university student working two part-time jobs to pay for their fees to get them through their education.

Beginning with a fork

If you get offered a job at the beginning of your career by a friend or acquaintance the fork always means a choice or some influence coming into your life to enhance your career, usually from the Mount of Luna.

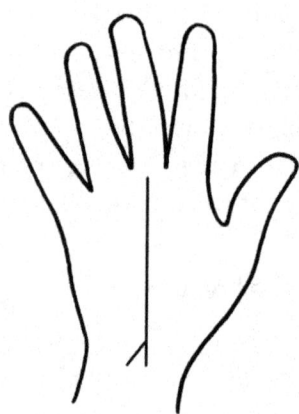

Fate line beginning with a fork

When the line from Luna touches, but goes through the fate line to the other side, this is a negative sign. This is a crisis point and a life changing situation, eg someone comes into your life like a business partner, but then takes all of the funds with them. It can also be someone you meet through work, that you marry, or is a major influence in your career and life, and you decide to change career paths altogether for more personal satisfaction rather than financial stability.

Beginning before the head line

We all don't know what we want to do in life, which is very common and not all of us are influenced by family or friends. But when the line appears around the middle of the palm, before the head line, we start to enjoy more freedom, balance and stability, and our chosen career path, or work, takes off, giving us a more comfortable lifestyle and deeper meaning and fulfilment, to our lives.

Scratchy or faint and strong

People who have scratchy or faint fate lines, can be gifted at what they do. These people can be doctors, lawyers, business executives, but can be living up to other people's expectations, which gives them a sense of not knowing who they really are. Because of this, they tend to get so busy making a living, they forget to make a life for themselves, and never get a sense of inner fulfilment and being at peace.

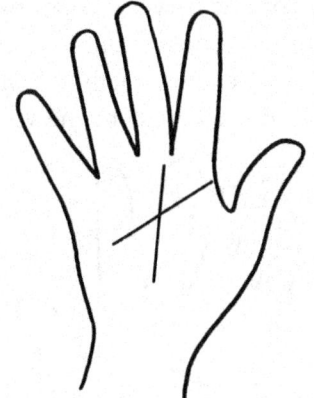

Fate line beginning in the middle before the head line

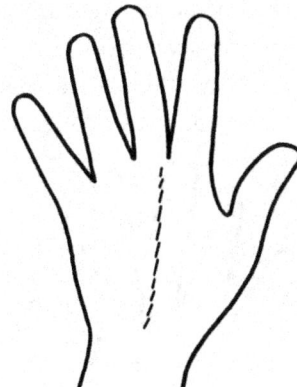

A scratchy fate line

A strong, deep fate line

Strong deep

This person knows who they are, and is always self-sufficient and independent. They can be quite dominating at times as they feel it is them against the world. There are issues with control, and so they like to do things their own way and achieve what they want out of life.

Ending at the head line

A fate line that ends at the head line is when people lose their sense of where they are going and feel lost. This can be due to unforeseen circumstances, unemployment, the death of a loved one, retrenchment or some mid-life crisis that makes them question their career or life path. When the head line has been touched by the fate line, this is around the age of thirty-forty years. After the ending of the fate line, some people may go from job to job, searching for meaning and fulfilment, others will always feel out of place, never settling down.

Ending at the heart line

When the fate line touches the heart line, this occurs around the ages between fifty and sixty, these people have stayed in their line of work for their entire lives. It can be said that these people enjoy the same habit, routines and behaviours. Change or diversity is something that's worth running away from. The tried and tested wins out here and the methodical way is what one wants, no matter how many people they found emotionally disturbing, they stayed the course to the very end.

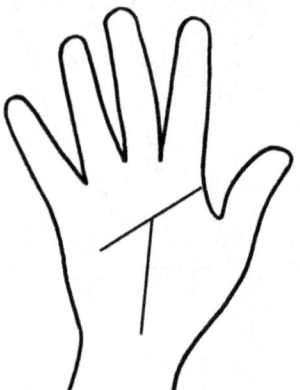 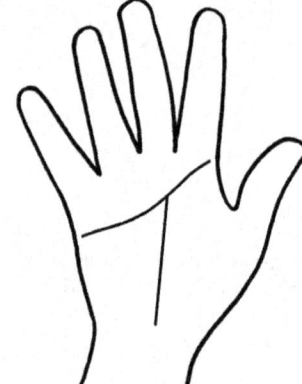

Fate line ending at head line   Fate line ending at the heart line

Breaks

If you have a break visible on your fate line, this can be an interruption, good or bad, and it could mean the loss of a job or getting a better job with more pay and a better lifestyle. If the fate line is stronger after the break, it's a positive sign, but if it fades out or becomes fainter, the break was a negative turning point in your life.

Islands

If you have an island on your fate line, stress and confusion about what direction to take with your career or life is visible at this time. This can lead to a feeling of emptiness and dissatisfaction at work and in life generally.

Just a note, the more palms I read, especially today, the fewer fate lines I see. I believe this is due to more jobs and careers becoming available, which is leading to mass confusion on a grand scale. This makes it difficult for the future generations coming through. Sometimes being spoilt for choice isn't such a good thing.

QUIZ TIME QUESTIONS

1. What does it mean when your fate line ends on your head line?
2. What does it mean when your fate line ends under the index/Jupiter finger?
3. If you don't have a fate line, what does that mean?
4. If your fate line commences on the Mount of Luna, will you like working with the public?
5. If your fate line is attached or begins within the life line, will you work in a family business or a career your parents have chosen?
6. If a fate line commences near the wrist and ends under a finger, what does this mean?
7. What does it mean if you've got a faint or scratchy fate line?
8. What does a break mean on the fate line?
9. If there is a fork at the beginning of the fate line, what does that mean?
10. What age would you be, if your fate line ends at the head line?

Answers:

1. A career or job that ends due to unforeseen circumstances, retrenchment, illness, death of a loved one. **2.** This person is ambitious and usually works for themselves. They can be a specialist as well, such a doctor, lawyer or surgeon. **3.** They like to follow their own paths and march to the beat of their own drum. They usually live an unconventional lifestyle. **4.** Yes, they enjoy working with people, always in the public eye and enjoy change and travel, and usually against what their parents wanted for them. **5.** Yes, they work in a family business or a chosen career picked by their parents. **6.** This person knew very early what they wanted to do and followed the correct path to achieve this reality. **7.** These people are living up to the expectations of others. Gifted doctors, lawyers, surgeons, but they burn the candle at both ends, looking for validation, but never really being satisfied. **8.** It's an interruption in this person's working life, and can be a positive sign, depending on what happens after the break. If it is a strong line after it's positive, if it's weak it's a negative sign. **9.** You have a choice of a job or a certain career at the beginning of your working life. **10.** Thirty to forty years of age.

HEALTH LINE

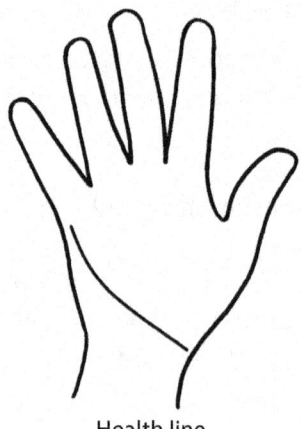

Health line

In palmistry, this line is called the Mercury line, Hepatic line or the Liver line. But to make it easier for you to remember, we'll call it the health line. The easiest way to locate this line is to trace it down from underneath the little/ Mercury finger. The line differs from the fate and Apollo line, as it leans diagonally across and not vertically down like the others. It usually touches the life line or just off it.

The health line relates to the stomach region with its many imbalances in digestion, feeling bloated, unsettled feelings with its aches and liver difficulties. It also represents your business skills, and how good you are in your own business or how well you go in the career you have chosen.

Laddered

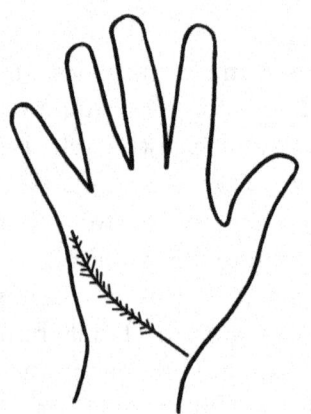

Laddered health line

When the line is in a ladder-like formation, you'll have digestive problems of some sort. Having an allergy test done aids in the process of elimination of what doesn't agree with you. The amount of colourings, flavourings and additives in the foods we digest, this puts our digestive systems under a lot of stress, causing difficulties here. The majority of you will find your body won't be able to absorb dairy, wheat or sugar well. These food intolerances create stomach ailments until certain foods have been eliminated, from your diet.

Business people with the laddered health line always run into difficulties. Stops and starts and deals never run smoothly.

Long, straight and deeply cut

Long, straight and deep health line

Some health problems may be indicated with the liver, as it may not be functioning as well as it should be. People with this line formation are aware of eating the right foods, but at times, overdo their intake of supplements, and this causes stress on the liver and the digestive process and bloating is the outcome.

This long, straight health line is found on many natural healers, reiki practitioners, massage therapists, especially when the line forms a clear triangle in the centre of the palm, with the head and the heart lines all connected. I have found some people who possess this line to often be psychic and have mediumistic abilities.

When it comes to business, most of the time they can be quite successful, having an innate ability to make the right decision at the right time. This is quite a fortunate sign to have on your hand.

Split by little lines

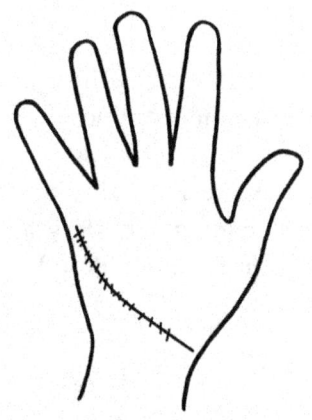

Lines intersecting the health line

When this line is intersected by small lines, you'll suffer from migraines or tension headaches. These lines are seen as outside influences affecting the everyday running of the business, causing stress and inner conflict for you, bringing on those headaches, and tension in the neck.

Islands

When there are islands detected on the health line, respiratory problems are the result. There can be issues such as bronchitis, pneumonia and inflammation of the throat are often present.

In business, confusion and delays with the everyday running of the business, money troubles occur with not enough money coming in and this puts a financial burden on you.

Breaks

Breaks on the health line aren't a good sign for anyone to have, and indicate overall stress on the stomach, digestive problems, liver not functioning as well as it should be, due to a stress overload, and not getting adequate rest or sufficient healthy food to strengthen your immune system.

If you own your own business, a termination of the business is indicated here, and a new change in your job will be most likely.

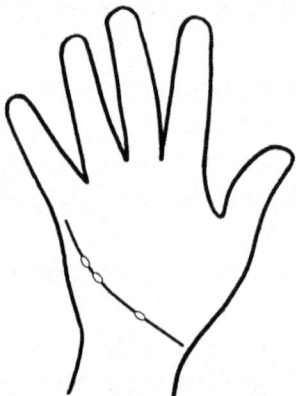 

Islands on the health line   Breaks on the health line

Missing health line

Always a favourable sign, as there will be no stomach complaints, and usually you will be someone who takes fitness to the extreme, enjoying a healthy, well-proportioned eating regime.

Business isn't a concern for you as you like to leave that up to those around you and your focus is on maintaining a healthy and strong constitution, letting you enjoy a happy and healthy lifestyle.

QUIZ TIME QUESTIONS

1. There are three other names the health line goes by, what are they?
2. What does this line relate to?
3. When the line is laddered, what does this mean?
4. In business, what does the laddered formation mean?
5. When the health line is absent, is this a fortunate sign?
6. Does business mean a lot to someone who doesn't have a health line?

Minor lines

7. If you have a strong, deep health line, would you be successful in business?
8. What health complaints are present when small intersecting lines are on the health line?
9. Does business run smoothly for someone with islands on their health line, and what health conditions could they have?
10. For a business owner, what does a break indicate when this occurs on the health line?

Answers:

1. The Hepatic, mercury and liver line. **2.** Digestive and stomach, liver and business difficulties. **3.** Indicates digestive problems or liver complaints. **4.** A lot of stops and starts with business and career, and trials and tribulations are a common occurrence. **5.** Yes, generally great health. **6.** No, they are more concerned and focused with exercise and eating well. **7.** Yes, these people can be quite successful, due to having a brilliant mind for business. **8.** Migraines and tension headaches. **9.** No, a lot of confusion and set-backs for business owners, or in your chosen career. Lungs, chest and throat tend to be a common issue with people who have islands. **10.** The termination of a business or chosen career is indicated and a new beginning with work at the time of the break.

LINE OF APOLLO

There are many names for this vertical line found underneath the ring/Apollo finger. It has been called the line of brilliance and the sun line.

Are you a happy, positive person? Do you enjoy life? Do you have creative artistic ability, enjoying the arts to all of its splendour? If you've answered yes to these questions, you most probably will have some form of this line underneath the ring/Apollo finger. Many people are found not to have this line, but have small traces of the line found in fragmented form under the ring/Apollo finger in some way.

Short bar at the heart line

Short bar at heart line

For the majority of people who I've read for, they have a short bar commencing at the heart line. These people have found contentment and inner happiness through hobbies and creative pursuits. They have the ability to love themselves in what they are doing, which brings them inner peace and satisfaction past retirement.

Apollo line at the head line

This line can also be found starting at the head line, at around the age of thirty-forty years. This indicates letting go of what others think you embrace your creative and inner talents, passion and enthusiasm take over your life and success and recognition follows in the field that excites you.

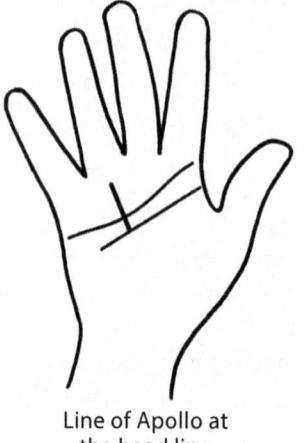

Line of Apollo at the head line

Clear long and well defined

These people have known for a very long time, what creative outlets they've wanted to pursue and they find success along the way. They are very creative and artistic, and their charisma and outlook on life is intoxicating. When I've read for people who have this clear long line, you can't but be caught up in a trance of their brilliance. Their auras shine like the sun, and their Apollo lines end in a fork which indicates wealth and acclaim.

Well defined and clear line of Apollo

Apollo line ending in a fork

Minor lines

Ending at head line

Some people that I've read for, their Apollo line began at the wrist, but ended at the head line. These people have become frustrated and have given up their creative pursuits, due to families, looking for full-time work and security. Unfortunately the joy and inner contentment they once had gets replaced with being serious, fulfilling their duty and the responsibility of living life.

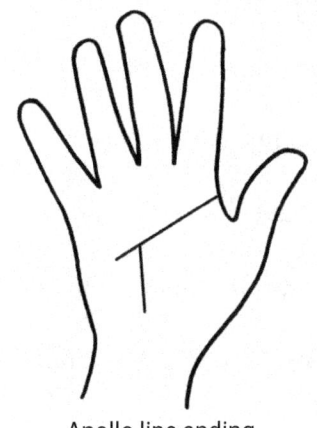

Apollo line ending at the head line

They must not give up this creative outlet and love, it's the blood that runs through their veins, and they need to hold on and find the time as it's their heart's joy. The inner joy for life is about expression of what is loved and sharing it with everyone else.

Rare lines

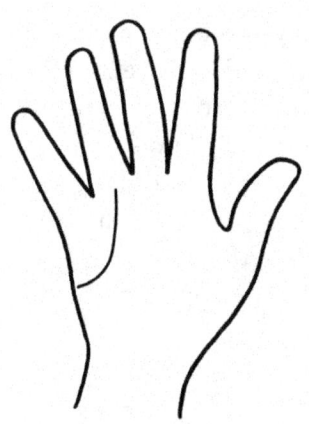

Rare Apollo line

My brother, David, has this line. It begins on the edge of percussion, and is a curve that goes towards the ring/Apollo finger. They tend to enjoy and have a talent for visual balance, line and shape, colours and what appeals to the eye. Self-development books and mind power workshops appeal to them as well. Photographers have this line, but only the successful ones who become recognised for their work.

If you don't have an Apollo line just yet, begin a creative pursuit or a hobby where you can channel your artistic ability. Within time an Apollo line will become visible. The lines on our hands aren't fixed, they come and go depending on what you do with your life. Take the step and reignite the spark of your creativity and share your brilliance with everybody.

QUIZ TIME QUESTIONS

1. To what does the Apollo line relate?
2. Under what finger will this line be located?
3. How many other names does the Apollo line have?
4. Is having a fork at the end of it a favourable sign?
5. When found commencing at the heart line, will enjoying retirement be more pleasurable?
6. At what age does the Apollo line begin when found on the head line?
7. When the line ends at the head line, what occurs for the line to terminate?
8. Where does the rare sun line begin?
9. Do all hands have an Apollo line?
10. Can you make an Apollo line appear on your hand?

Answers:

1. Happiness, creativity, fame and inner contentment. **2.** Ring/Apollo finger. **3.** The sun line, the line of brilliance and the inner realm line. **4.** Yes, a fortunate sign usually fame and recognition. **5.** Yes, they find inner happiness through their hobbies and creative pursuits after retirement. **6.** Between the ages of thirty-forty. **7.** The starting of a family, work, responsibility, duty and responsibility of looking after a family financially. **8.** On the side of the hand at percussion and curves upwards towards the ring/Apollo finger. **9.** No. **10.** Yes, you can, begin your creative pursuits and watch the Apollo line appear before your very eyes.

NINE
Timing

> The most important truth we can know is within us,
> not outside of us, and it is us. — *MYNZAH OSIRIS*

The majority of Palmists like to divide the head, heart and life lines into two equal parts from the beginning of each line to the very end. For a more accurate reading, I've found that dividing the line into equal parts of seven to give a more precise probability, as the body and its regeneration period changes every seven years.

Life

The quickest way to find the time on the life line is to draw vertical lines from the base of the index/Jupiter and middle/Saturn fingers until they hit the life line. So, a line from the middle of the index/Jupiter finger to the life line is ten. Between the index/Jupiter and the middle/Saturn finger is the age of twenty, and the middle of the middle/Saturn finger vertically straight down to the life line is thirty-five years of age. After that line has been drawn, divide the rest of the life line into seven years until the end of the life line.

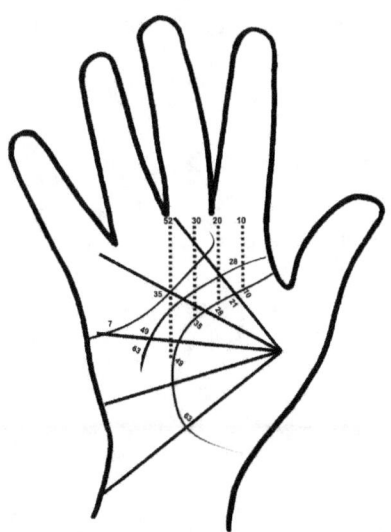

Timing calculation

Know Thyself: The Insightful Art of Palmistry

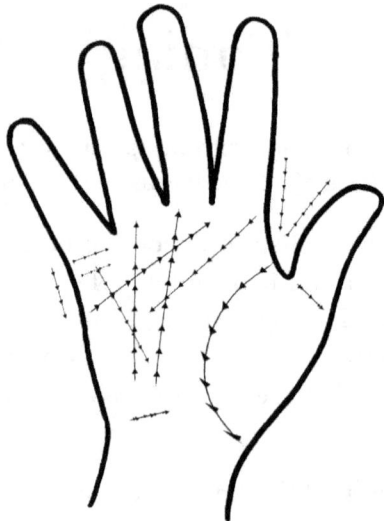

Time flow

Measuring time on the life line

With the heart and head lines begin measuring the time from where the lines begin as seen in the diagram. Start seven year intervals, fourteen, twenty-one until the end of the line.

I have found using this method to be the best way to get a good probability of all occurrences seen on their three major lines.

TEN
The Mounts

> To know yourself, you must first sacrifice the illusion that already you do. — *VIRONIKA TUGALEVA*

You can get a really quick description of yourself the moment you take a glimpse of the palm of your hand. The mounts are the fleshy pads of skin located in eight positions, some noticeable, others non-existent. When you see a standout mount on your palm, this is an indication of where your energies are focused.

The mounts are ruled by various planets, just like your fingers. Remember, when looking at your palm, to ignore anything average, but look at what shouts out at you, wanting your attention.

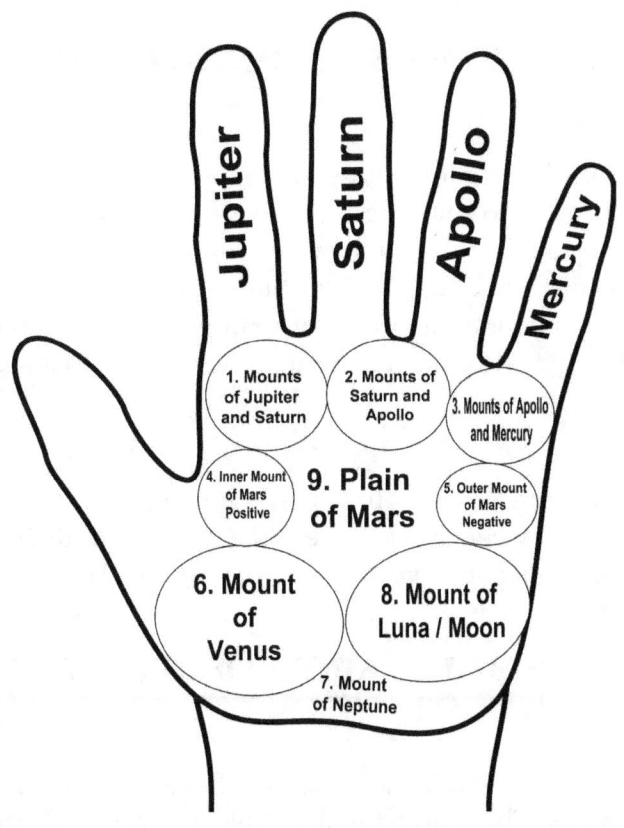

The mounts of the hand

MOUNT ONE: JUPITER/SATURN

High

This person is confident and ambitions, they can be a great leader as they like to take charge and make decisions for others. Goal setting and attaining what they set themselves means a lot to them, and they possess good minds for business as they're very reliable, logical and practical. At times, they can push themselves too much, taking life to the extremes, and becoming over self-involved, serious and domineering.

Flat

This person will be shy and timid, with no self-confidence. They tend to be lazy, insecure with a careless type of attitude, and with little concern for anyone or anything. Usually, these people are drifters who never really fit in.

MOUNT TWO: SATURN/APOLLO

High

This person takes their duty and responsibility very seriously, especially when it comes to their creative and artistic endeavours. They enjoy time alone and like to finish what they start. They are always talented in some creative field, and literally turn their hobby or interest into a full-time job due to perserverance and commitment to their craft. These people enjoy the beauty in everything that catches their eyes and imagination.

Flat

When this area is flat, this person will not care too much for beauty or art, and having any culture won't be at the forefront of their interests. They usually are quite negative, suffering from melancholy with no real zest for life or having fun.

MOUNT THREE: APOLLO/MERCURY

High

This person is creative and has a great way of expressing themselves, usually with words. They can be gifted public speakers and have an ability to entrance or capture their audience through their creative expression. From what I've found, romance and sexual communication is very important to these people, and they enjoy working in communications, such as freelance writers for magazines, media and public relation roles, as they have a great skill with words and an extensive vocabulary. They can be great at business, but at times are known to extend the truth due to their ability with words and telling stories.

Flat

Expressing and communicating isn't one of their greatest talents, so they can become very frustrated and irritable most of the time. Often they're found in unconventional relationships due to their sexual immaturity, and most of the time they lack patience and sympathy for others.

MOUNT FOUR: THE INNER MOUNT OF MARS (POSITIVE)

This is located between the Mount of Jupiter and the Mount of Venus.

Thick

This person has a lot of physical courage and stamina, fighting for what they believe in and most of the time they'll stick up for the underdog. They rarely get sick and if they do it's not for very long. Most of the time they work for the emergency services, such as the ambulance, police, fire and rescue, army, airforce and navy. They usually enjoy doing martial arts as a hobby and like to be seen as rescuers, for those in need.

Flat

This person will stay out of the lime light and avoid confrontation at all costs. Physical courage isn't a strong point and quite often they are seen as loners.

MOUNT FIVE: THE OUTER MOUNT OF MARS (NEGATIVE)

Location – Fleshy pad between the Mount of Mercury and the Mount of the Moon/Luna

Thick

This person has strong beliefs and ideals. They have plenty of moral courage and will stick up for what they believe in, e.g.: religion, family, politics. At times, they can take it to extremes and need to learn how to know when enough is enough.

Flat

This person is very impressionable and can be a pushover. They find it hard to stick by their convictions and can be easily persuaded by others.

MOUNT SIX: THE MOUNT OF VENUS

Location –The fleshy mount underneath the thumb which is enclosed by the life line.

Thick

When the mount is high, this person is friendly and outgoing, easily enjoying the company of others. They're sympathetic to other's needs, love music and have a strong, healthy sex drive. There is always an abundance of energy, zest and vitality to enjoy life's wonders.

Flat

These people usually don't have energy or vitality by the bucket loads and are always sick. They've got a poor constitution and enjoy their own company. They don't know how to relate to others and most of the time can be seen as cold fish, due to having poor relationships skills and lack of energy. They very often have or suffer from a poor libido.

MOUNT SEVEN: MOUNT OF NEPTUNE

Location - in between the Mounts of Luna and Venus, near the wrist.

Thick

This person who has a thick Mount of Neptune, has a great intuitive ability. They always follow their heart and most of the time are correct. This mount is the gateway between the conscious and sub-conscious selves. Anyone who has a thick mount here are logical and rational, but also creative and intuitive at the same time. These people are very compassionate and loving towards everyone and thing.

Hollow

These people aren't in touch with what they want out of life. I have found there is a lot of inner tension in their lives. They always feel like something is missing, but they are not sure what it is. By having more fun and alone time, will bring out what they want most close to their hearts. It is available but they must be prepared to listen. Being in solitude each day and quieting the mind will bring about inner peace, and the answers to which they seek to live a more happy meaningful life.

MOUNT EIGHT: THE MOUNT OF THE MOON/LUNA

Location – the fleshy mount on the outer edge of the palm (percussion) below the Mount of Mars negative.

Thick

This person has a strong imagination, artistic ability and is intuitively gifted, especially when there are vertical lines on the mount. I've also found this person to enjoy being around the water, beaches, lakes, rivers, dams, which have a soothing effect on them, bringing them back into the moment. With these people, vivid dreams and precognitions about what may happen next in their lives or those around them come to fruition often. They make great psychics.

Lovers of travel, music and poetry, if there are lots of horizontal lines on this mount, travels overseas are indicated. They are very much into the mystical part of life, looking for signs and omens. They are very much aware of what is going on in their inner lives, which most of the time is very rich and rewarding.

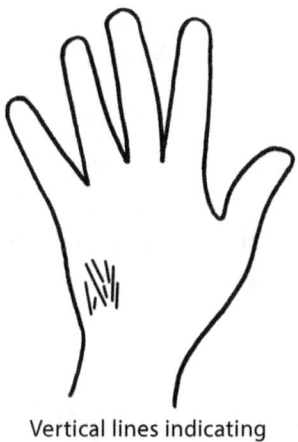

Vertical lines indicating strong intuition

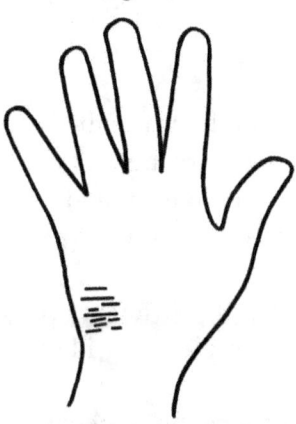

Horizontal lines indicating overseas travel

Flat

These are very rational people, who like to disapprove of everything you say until they experience it for themselves. They lack imagination or an open mind as everything is black or white, without any shades of grey. These people are straight down the line.

Lower mount of moon/Luna

When the Mount of Luna is positioned a little bit lower than the Mount of Venus, this person is very sensitive. The can pick up if there is tension in a room, or between two people in a relationship. They don't like noisy environments, loud or obnoxious people. They tend to feel overwhelmed and drained at times due to their sensitivities. They enjoy their time alone and like-minded people just like themselves.

MOUNT NINE: THE PLAIN OF MARS

Location - the centre of the palm.

Thick

This person is self-confident and knows what they want out of life, always self-reliant, but at times can be quite tactless with the way they go about getting what they want, as they can be seen as quite forceful and domineering.

Flat

This person is always timid and shy, needing reassurance from those around them. They never feel like they belong and most of the time feel like loners.

Percussion

Location – from the outside of the palm, underneath the little/Mercury finger all the way down the wrist. What we are looking for here is how creative you are, and where your curve is located, as the locations of the curve mean different ways you go about expressing your creativity.

Position 1: When the curve is underneath the little/Mercury finger. You have great creativity and imagination, with plenty of ideas and insights, but don't act on them.

Position 2: When the curve is in the middle location of percussion, you can turn your ideas into reality through your own efforts.

Position 3: When the curve is down the bottom of percussion, near the wrist, you can turn your ideas and insights into reality which produce lasting results for you, eg a successful business.

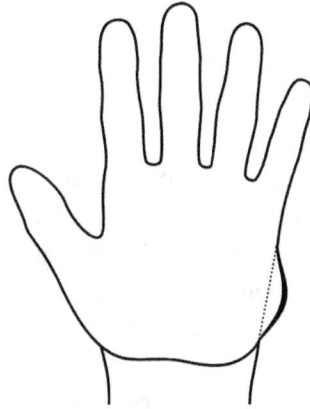

A curve on percussion in the third position near the wrist. Manifesting dreams into a reality.

QUIZ TIME QUESTIONS

1. Would you say a person with a high Jupiter/Saturn mount would be shy and a loner?
2. Would a person with a high mount of Saturn/Apollo be seen as lazy with no artistic ability?
3. If a person has a flat mount of Saturn/Apollo, would they be full of energy and life?
4. Does a person with a high Apollo/Mercury mount great at expressing themselves with words?
5. What work environments would you find a person with a high Apollo/Mercury mount in?
6. If a flat mount is found under Apollo/Mercury, would they be involved in an unconventional relationship?
7. Does a person with a flat mount of Mars positive enjoy confrontation?
8. If you have a thick mount of Venus, would you be empathetic and have a strong sex drive?
9. When the mount of Luna is thick, would you enjoy being by the water?
10. If a person has a thick mount of Neptune, would they be extremely intuitive?

Answers:

1. No, these people are very self-confident and ambitious, they like to lead others. **2.** No, they have a lot of discipline and duty always with work on their minds. They are always talented in some creative way. **3.** No, they usually have little energy or vitality at all. They can be seen as quite negative and down. **4.** Yes, communication is what they're great at, especially with words. **5.** Newspaper, freelance writer for magazines, public relations and media. **6.** Yes, most of the time due to sexual immaturity, look for the low-set little/Mercury finger. **7.** No, they like to stay out of the lime light. Courage isn't one of their strong points. **8.** Yes, a lover of people with a good heart and a strong healthy sex drive. **9.** Yes, being in or around water, the beach, creek, waterfall, really relaxes people with a thick mount of Luna. **10.** Definitely, always listening to their first impressions, as they are correct.

ELEVEN

Bars, Markings and Signs

He has no need for faith who knows the uncreated, who has cut off rebirth, who has destroyed any opportunity for good or evil, and cast away all desire. He is indeed the ultimate man. — GAUTAMA BUDDHA

What I'm about to describe to you and show you, won't be on everyone's hands. Some on the other hand, no pun intended, will be shown in their true and correct form. The stronger and more developed the sign, the deeper and more meaningful it will be, and for the weaker, partial or fainter the line, the less the impact the marking will have. These markings will give you a further in-depth view of your talents and abilities. As well as a few challenges, you may have which you can remedy by being aware of them and correcting.

Remember to look at both of your hands, to see if you are working on and developing your talents to this very day, and these signs will be strong on both hands, if this is the case. If these signs are on your dominant hand, after twenty-one, but not on your passive hand, which are the talents and challenges given to you by biological factors and inheritance. You have worked hard on your skills and strengthened your weaknesses with discipline and determination, through your own efforts and action, to live out your dreams and visions.

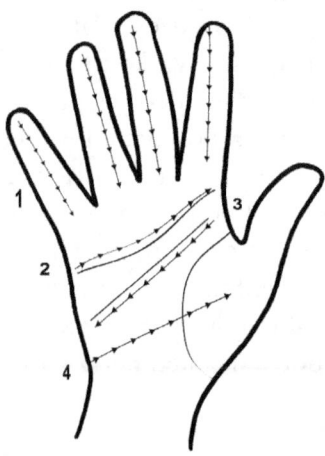

The Reading Pattern for these markings and signs on your hand

I will be writing about these signs and markings with a net pattern for you to follow, so you won't be scattered or miss any important information. I have learnt through experience that this is the best way to go.

The pattern will be as follows, from the finger tips down, then working from the top of the palm, left to right, then right to left through the middle of the palm, then left to right along the base of the palm of the hand.

Bars on the finger tips

When you see little horizontal lines on your finger tips or thumb, this is stress and frustration in your life, depending on which finger they appear. Example, lines on your index/Jupiter finger relate to your work, career and self-confidence. Lines appearing on your ring/Apollo finger can relate to you not being able to channel your creativity in the right way. While lines on you little/Mercury finger, can be frustration and anxiety in a relationship, or sexual difficulty. These lines can also mean a hormonal imbalance, like menopause. If these situations go on for too long, they'll appear on the bottom phalanges as well, after due time.

Until you work out a way to overcome stress and frustration, by taking up meditation or an exercise regime to release and let go, this inner tension will continue.

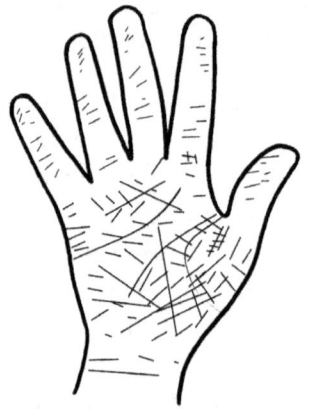

Stress lines on the finger tips and lower phalanges and palm of a nervous person's hand. Better known as the full hand.

Affection line

Usually these little lines are called marriage lines, but I have found they don't always mean that. Some people who have these lines, have never been married before, but are committed in a relationship that is important to them. Example, a spinster who has a deep relationship with her niece, or a bachelor who treats his nephew like the son he always wanted, and sometimes it can be career minded people who are married to their job. Where there is a real passion there for them.

From what I have noticed, the more important the relationship, the deeper and longer the line. The majority of people have a couple of these lines. In times gone by, and even now, most palmists, will look to tell you how many times you will be married, and how many children you'll have. But in my experience, children lines and how many times you will be married is false, and is not warranted here.

Absent

Now, if there is not one line to be seen, you may have an inability to commit to someone or something you care about. You may

Bars, markings and signs

like to cater for your own needs and wants. Some people may see you as self-important or selfish, but it is better to have what makes you happy, than be miserable.

Clear and straight

Clear and straight

This relationship is very important to you. The relationship or connection brings a lot of happiness and inner fulfilment into your life. You may be very committed to your career or some type of interest that you're passionate about.

Ends in a fork

You maybe still in your relationship or career physically, but emotionally and mentally, you left a long time ago. Usually there's been a broken commitment or loss of interest, and you have started to look elsewhere for happiness. In the end, there will be a separation of this union.

Ending in a fork

Curves down touching heart line

This is called the divorce line. Most of the time, you get into the habit of connecting with the wrong people or work. In days gone by, it was called the widow line. Back in days of old, if you got divorces or your partner died, you never remarried, but it is a lot different today, with the throw-away society we live in. The average marriage in Australia lasts twelve years.

Runs up underneath the little/ Mercury finger

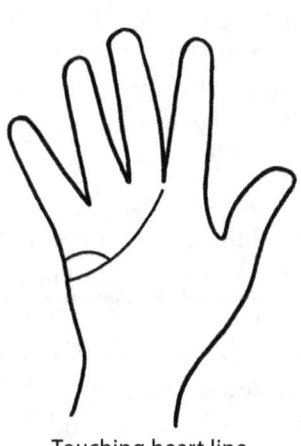
Touching heart line

When this happens, it has to do with an inhibition of a sexual nature. I have seen this on people who have not had sex for a long duration of time, or fear intimacy.

Parallel lines

This person has a very strong commitment to someone and their career at the same time, or a child comes along and they become extra committed to the child and their partner as well. It doesn't mean that someone is being unfaithful and having something on the side, but two strong connections side by side.

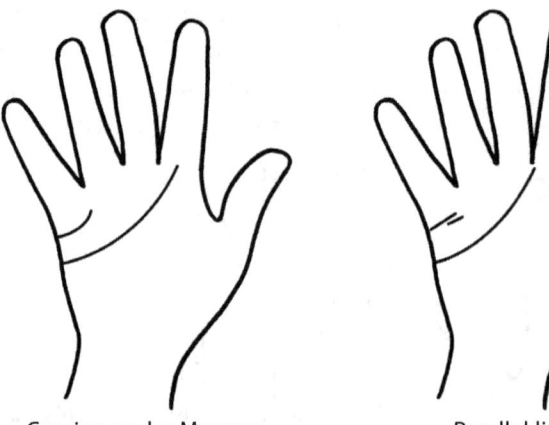

Curving under Mercury   Parallel lines

Medical stigmata

Usually three or four small vertical lines on the Apollo/Mercury mount, are referred to as the medical stigmata or the Samaritan lines. These people, by nature, are nurturers and healers. They enjoy helping and caring for people. Most of the time they are found in people who are in the alternative therapies, massage, homeopathy, chiropractic and acupuncture. I've also seen doctors, nurses and dentists with these markings. If you are not in these working fields, you may at some point be looking at studying in these fields as you've got talents here.

Not all people who have these markings may be gifted in healing people, but they do like to look out and help

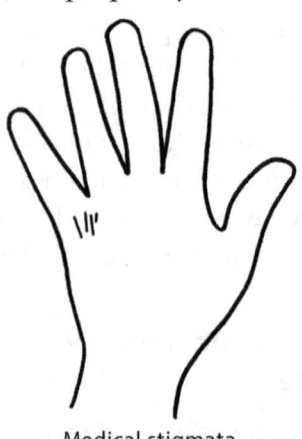

Medical stigmata

people in need. For instance, you go away and a neighbour puts your bins out or collects your mail, or you get sick and they make chicken soup for you. These people are empathetic and loving. They go out of their way to help those around them.

Mark of a teacher

Mark of a teacher

There are two small lines that are located on the Mercury/Apollo mount. One of the little lines is vertical, and the one next to it is a diagonal line. If you have this, you know how to get the best out of people by raising the bar on their strengths, and making them believe in themselves. You can use your creativity to open up the minds to those in front of you. These people don't always stand up in front of a classroom, but appear to you when you need the encouragement and shove to get you moving.

Passion line

Passion line

If you are into swinging and not off branches, partner swapping, living out your sexual fantasies with your partner or strangers, these people definitely like the lights on in the bedroom. They have a heightened sexual appetite.

This line starts from the heart line, usually about midline, and crosses diagonally in between the ring/Apollo and little/Mercury fingers, or underneath the little/Mercury finger itself. If you have this line, you must find you partner physically attractive and for it to work, their partner must enjoy visual erotica and sexual fantasy.

I once read for a very attractive lady who had this, which stood out a mile on her hands. The first thing I said to her was that sex is never boring, and she looked at me and said, "Not on your life." Are you all looking for this line? I bet you are.

The girdle of Venus

Girdle of Venus

This line runs above the heart line in a curve in its proper form from the middle/Saturn finger to the ring/Apollo finger. It can be seen in a few disguises, a fine horizontal line or a couple of lines above the heart line, or from underneath the middle/Saturn finger all the way out to the percussion side of the palm, underneath the little/Mercury finger.

The bearer of this line is emotionally sensitive to people, the environment and to life in general. These people like to escape the monotony of life by going into the imaginary world, where they seek colour and excitement. They are usually talented artistically, writers, actors, poets, painters and spiritual travellers looking for Nirvana. Art galleries, museums, the theatre or going out to a good restaurant with like-minded individuals is what they enjoy most. They are not the conventional type, and like to do things differently from those around them. In their love lives, they are very flirtatious and passionate, and they have a lot of emotional energy to channel. If this energy isn't released, they become very moody and highly strung. When the Girdle of Venus is made up of two or three lines, this person takes all of these qualities to the extreme, and they may escape life through drugs, alcohol or risky

Long Girdle of Venus

Girdle of Venus made up of three lines which amplify the Girdle's qualities

Bars, markings and signs

Ring of Saturn

Ring of Solomon

Ring of Solomon double

sexual behaviour, especially if they have a lowset, long little/Mercury finger with a large space between the little/Mercury and ring/Apollo fingers, and a large Mount of Venus.

Ring of Saturn

If you have a semicircular ring underneath the middle/Saturn finger, you will take duty, and responsibility seriously, and often become too serious about life in general. You need to relax, let go and reclaim the love of life. Go out and enjoy hobbies, interests that you once had and make life fun and enjoyable. Make the time to reclaim the balance as work and seriousness lead to life on your own, with no company.

Ring of Solomon

This marking will be seen above the teacher's square if you have one. It comes in two forms, a circle around the base of the index/Jupiter finger, or a diagonal line underneath the index/Jupiter finger. People who have this marking have the gift of natural insight into people, what moves them and the reasons they do the things they do. People fascinate and intrigue them. They are open-minded, empathetic and are great listeners, who don't have an aura of judgement about them. People naturally open up to them, as they have no ego and have a grace about them that lets people feel at ease with them when in their company. Successful psychologists, entrepreneurs, business executives and lawyers, have this mark. Teachers

129

who teach in an inspiring way have the ring of Solomon as well. If you have a double diagonal line of Solomon, you truly have an amazing gift and it should not be wasted, so go out and enlighten people using your knowledge and wisdom to inspire others.

Teacher's square

Here is another sign of the teacher. This time it is a square formed on the Mount of Jupiter, from an attached line rising from the life line. This is a great sign for someone who can make a lesson worth listening to. If you have this marking, you'll make a great teacher, instructor, manager or mentor. You just have a natural way of explaining or getting through to people which makes them understand and listen, you are a naturally gifted teacher.

Mystic cross

Now moving into the middle of the palm in between the heart and head line, if a cross appears here, this is known as the Mystic Cross, or the La Croix Mystique. These people look for signs, omens and synchronicity. Definitely not caught up in the analytical, rational, practical part of life, they usually have a tarot deck or Angel cards on them or around the house, to which they go to ask for answers to questions on a regular basis. They do enjoy the esoteric, anything that's hidden away from the mainstream media or daily life. They enjoy discussing and reading about UFOs,

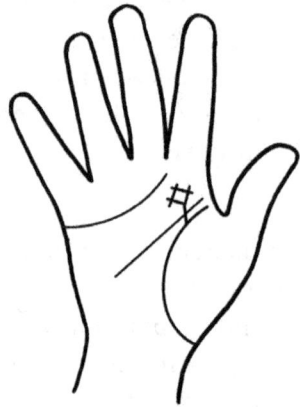

Teacher's square

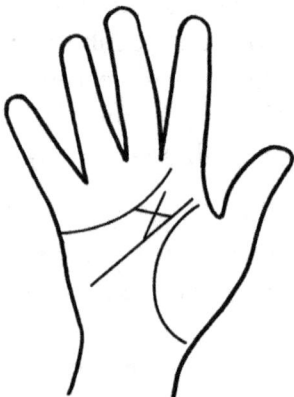

Single mystic cross

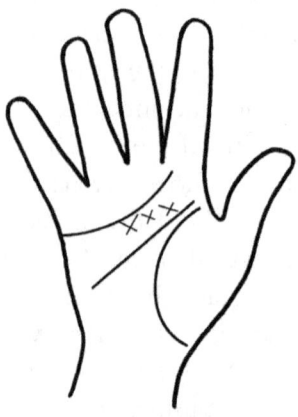

Triple mystic cross

conspiracy theories, the Illuminati, anything the majority of people don't want to discuss due to the fear of ridicule. They like to talk about these things and are open about them in the right company.

If there is more than one cross in between the heart and head line, this person is very much wrapped up into superstition. They like to belong to some type of group that works in the arcane arts, and very much enjoys and is fascinated by ghosts, goblins and ghouls.

Intuition line

Intuition or Spirit line

Now, I've only ever seen this on few people, so I believe it is a rare marking indeed. It's a curved line that begins on the Mount of Luna, and ends on the Mount of Mercury. They are a truly gifted psychic or medium. There are alot of not so gifted psychics and mediums out there. But if you happen to get a glimpse of the psychics hand before they give you a reading, and they have it, you are in for a treat, as they are the real deal.

I was once in a spiritual workshop and a lady from the class asked if I read palms, and I said that I did. Next minute, a lady from across the other side of the room's ears pricked up, and pushes her palms underneath my nose pushing everyone out of the way. In a strong, menacing tone she asked, "Can you tell me what this line is?" It was the intuition line, and I looked her straight in the eye and announced, you know what this line means. With a big smile on her face, and testing my skills, she departed as quickly as she had arrived. When lunch time came around, this lady gave me a reading for free, and it was one of the best readings I've ever had. Doris Stokes, the great English medium, possessed this intuition line, or spirit line.

Travel lines

These are the small lines that start on the percussion side on the Mount of Luna, and go all the way to the Mount of Mars, negative. The longer and deeper the line, the more the journey has a positive effect on your life experience.

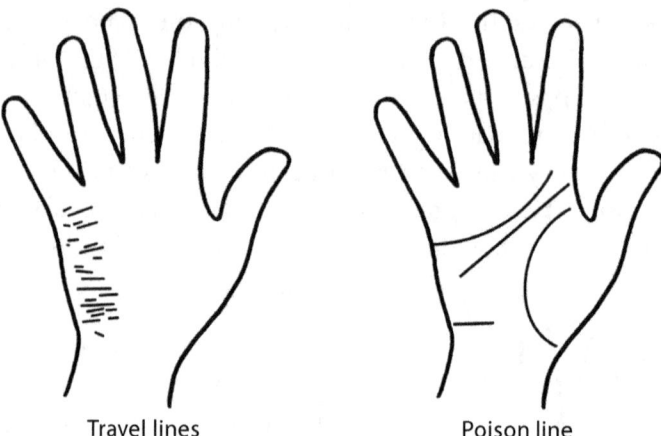

Travel lines   Poison line

Poison line

This is a straight bar line which is located on the Mount of Luna. People who have this line, which is usually about three centimetres in length, can become dependent on drugs. They can have a strong reaction to medications and become addicted, if the right one isn't prescribed. A lot more children these days have an over responsive immune system, which makes them react strongly to sugar, food additives, colourings, flavourings, and chemicals which are used to enhance foods and drinks.

From my own experiences, people who have a sensitive constitution, week life line, which is close to the thumb, and usually have a laddered health line. They have strong allergic reactions to food and drugs with stomach and digestion troubles. The best thing to do is get an allergy test from your doctor, to find out what your body reacts

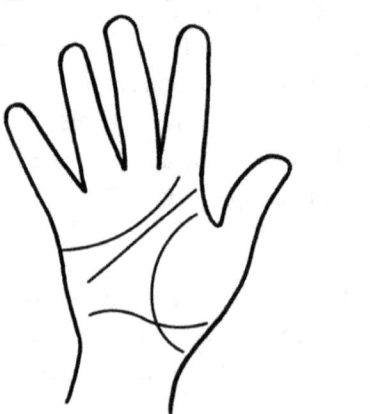 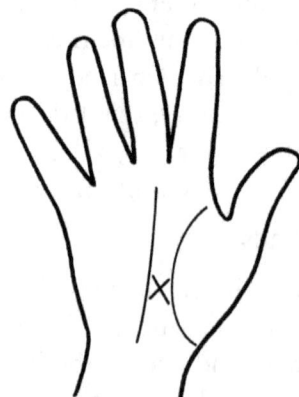

Via lascivia or line of escape   St Andrew's cross

strongly to and take it out of your healthy eating plan. Traditionally, this line was also called the Hypothenar Bar.

The via lascivia

When the line is longer and is curved in a small semicircular line that connects the Mount of Luna to the Mount of Venus. This is called the line of escape. People with this line escape the everyday hum-drum for the rush and stimulation and excitement that drugs, risqué behaviour, sky-diving and mountain climbing can provide.

St Andrew's cross

In between the fate line and the life line, there can be a cross. This is called the St Andrew's Cross and if you have it sometime in your life, you've saved the life of someone. It doesn't have to be physically, like from drowning, but you may have talked someone out of suicide. I have seen this marking on many counsellors. Once I saw five of these on a gentleman's hand and he worked as an emergency doctor for a very reputable hospital in Australia.

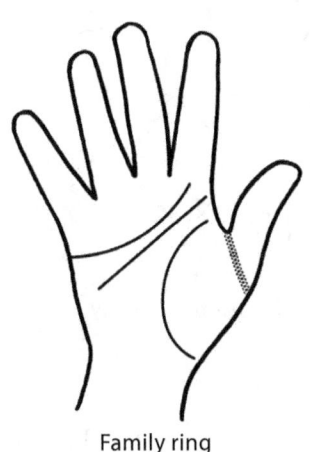

Family ring

The family ring

This is a vertical line at the base of the thumb. When this is present, you'll have strong connections with your family. You enjoy maintaining strong relationships with your blood ties. Some people who have this line, may be still dependent or receive support from their family, but if the line is present at the beginning, and absent about half way down through your life, you'll cut ties or become estranged from family members later in life.

Loyalty line

This is a deep cut line usually red in colour, which is connected to the family ring and crosses the Mount of Venus runs close to touching the life line. It shows a deep loyalty to this person, usually a family member, a cause, country, a favourite football team, which means everything to them.

Stress lines on Mount of Venus

When there are many lines running out from the thumb across to the Mount of Venus, there are influences that are close to you. These people cause you stress and annoy you.

If you have a few lines here that is fine, but an array of lines from the top of the Venus mount all the way down to the bottom of the life line are a continuous annoyance. This is usually from your family that you were brought up with throughout your life. When the horizontal stress line touches the life line, it will affect you in a way that causes you grief and frustration. If there are many lines on the top of Venus Mount, but none down the bottom, you had these annoyances in your life earlier on when you were younger, but as an adult, they are no longer present as you made the decision to stay away, which can be easier as you now love your family from a distance.

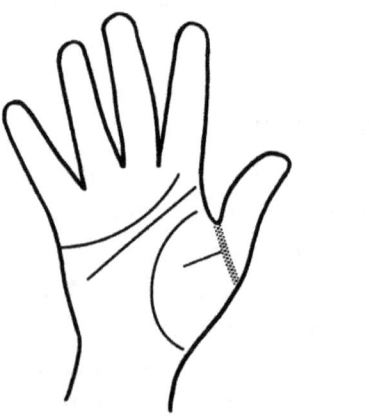

Loyalty line connected to the family ring

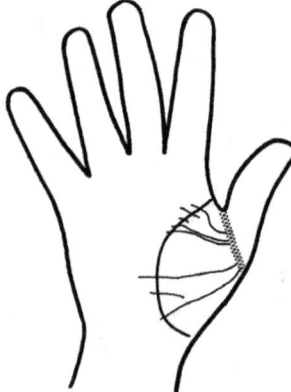

Lines of stress from family

Support lines

When there are lines running vertically down inside the life line, these are called support lines. These are the people in your life that help and guide you, nurturing your growth as an individual. Some are short, meaning this person is in your life for a short period of time, teaching you a lesson and then leaves short afterwards. Other lines might travel all the way down to the bottom of the life line and these people will stay with you your whole life. Some palmist believe that these lines are from people you knew who have passed over into

Bars, markings and signs

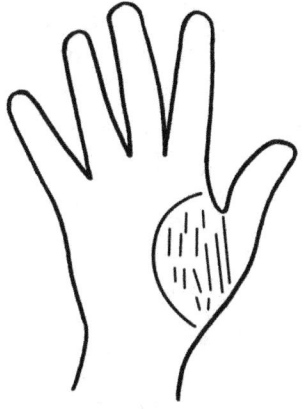
Support lines

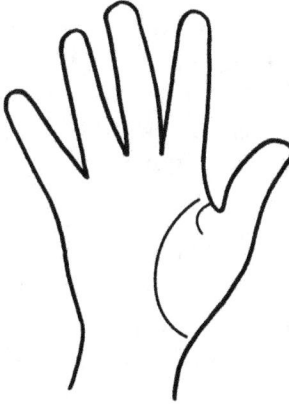
The Mars line

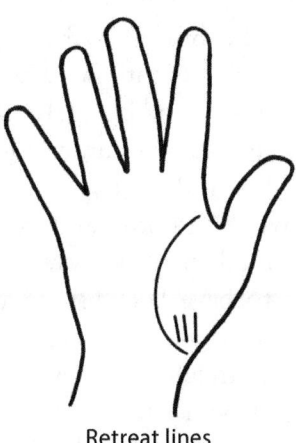
Retreat lines

the spirit world, and that are now your guardian angels helping you from the other side.

The line of Mars

This is a small line curved inside the life line on the Mount of Mars, positive. The line is usually about two centimetres in length. When it is found without any blemishes or splits, you can say that you've got plenty of drive and determination with a passion to excel. This line is found on intense people who are ready for action. I've seen this line on professional footballers, martial artists and people in the armed forces. These people always have a strong constitution and hardly ever get ill, especially if your line is strong and deeply cut.

Retreat lines

Two or three short clear lines inside the life line down at the base of Venus are called retreat lines. If you have these, you'll want to get away from the rat race and escape to the country, in a little cabin on some property, or a house by the water to get away from the hustle and bustle.

Rascette lines

Often referred to as the bracelets or Bracelets of Neptune, they are found on the wrist below the palm. There will usually be two or more bracelet lines, and when they are clear of any breaks or chains, it is an indication of good health and longevity. The more bracelets you have the longer your life.

If the first bracelet closest to your wrist is turned up in the middle and you are a female, you may have a problem with giving birth or conceiving a baby. So there can be an imbalance with your reproduction system. If you are a male, you may have an imbalance with your internal organs or testicles not being able to produce sperm.

Healthy rascette/bracelet lines

An imbalance with the reproductive system

Simian line

My beautiful little daughter, Zara, has this line formation. It is where the head and the heart lines merge into one line along the palm of the hand. It is very rare, especially when you have it on both hands. My daughter is now three years old and head lines have appeared underneath the simian line.

Due to the heart and head line being one, these people have a hard time knowing the difference between their thoughts and their feelings. So, they become very frustrated, emotional and are intense. These people run on instinct and belief. If you have this rare line, one in a hundred for one hand, and one in the tens of thousands if you have it on both hands, you will be truly gifted in some way, due to your ability to have laser like focus and tunnel vision to achieve what you want. You have so much determination and discipline to be a success at anything you do. Many people who have

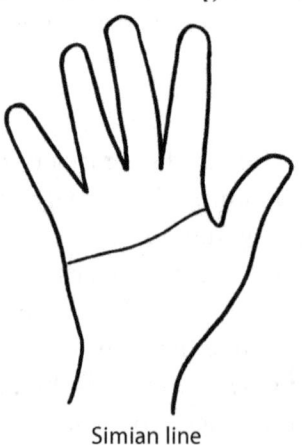
Simian line

Bars, markings and signs

Simian line with Girdle of Venus

this line find it hard to be logical and rational, because they are always full of excitement and enthusiasm. They don't stop. When you do something, you do it twice as hard as the next person. What you believe is always right and there is no in-between, because of this they can be seen as socially different to those around them due to a build-up of inner tension. You'll always feel something is always not quite right leaving you feel frustrated and agitated.

The best remedy for any inner tension is to channel this tension into a creative pursuit to calm and relax the body and mind. Henry Miller had a simian hand and his outlet was writing. Robert De Niro also has one as well, and he's one of the best male actors of this century. Tony Blair, England's past Prime Minister has this line. My beautiful little daughter likes to paint. When you find a creative endeavour that you enjoy, this outlet will release any pent up energy making you feel happier and content, which makes life fun and enjoyable.

Simian line with heart and head lines attached

When giving readings to simian handed people, I have noticed they have turned to religion in a big way. This probably gives them the peace of mind and inner stillness that God can give you. Pope John XXIII had a simian line and the founder of the Theosophical Society, Madame Blavatsky, the nineteenth century astrologer and occultist had one as well.

It has also been stated that simian line people, can be associated with heart defects, such as heart disease. So, it might be a good idea to stop smoking, becoming overweight or run too many marathons, as this all can be very taxing on your heart. This is not a certainty, but there is a chance especially with simian lined people for this to occur, so caution is advised and warranted.

QUIZ TIME QUESTIONS

1. Would you say a person with a Girdle of Venus is emotional or sensitive?
2. Would a person who works in a health profession, such as a doctor or marriage therapist, likely to possess the medical stigmata?
3. If you have bars on the tips of your fingers would you say that you've been stressed and frustrated?
4. Is the teacher's square located under the middle/Saturn finger?
5. If you have a ring of Solomon, does this give you an insight into people and how they think?
6. If you have a cross formation in between the heart and head line, would you enjoy the mystical part of life?
7. When you have a passion line, does this make you dull and boring in the bedroom?
8. When you have a straight bar, which is around two centimetres in length on the Mount of Luna. Could you have a strong reaction to drugs?
9. People with simian lines, are they gifted in some way, are they intense individuals?
10. Where is the Saint Andrew's Cross located. And what does it mean?

Answers:

1. Yes, they are very sensitive to people and their surroundings. **2.** Yes, most of the time. **3.** Yes, this is a sign of frustration or someone with a hormonal deficiency. **4.** No, it's located under the index/Jupiter finger. **5.** Yes, these people are fascinated and intrigued by people. They have great psychological insight. **6.** Yes, these people enjoy the mystical side of life, and look for messages or signs and omens throughout the day. **7.** Definitely not these people have a very good sexual imagination and have a heightened sexual appetite. **8.** Yes, these people have a strong reaction to drugs, and many may become dependent on them. **9.** People who have a simian line are always gifted in some way, due to them achieving success through their determination and discipline. They work twice as hard as anyone else to achieve their vision. They can be intense individuals. **10.** It's found in between the fate and life line, which is a cross formation. These people have saved someone's life physically or emotionally by talking them out of suicide.

TWELVE

Palm Prints

If you don't know yourself, you may easily blow away opportunities meant for success! Know who you are made of, and save your dreams from premature death. — ISRAELMORE AYIVOR

Just like the prints on the finger tips, we do have occasionally palm prints as well, whether underneath fingers, or maybe on the Mount of the Moon or Venus. Not all hands have palm prints, but for those of you who do. They give further depth to your personality.

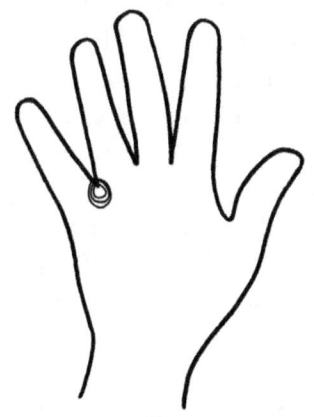

Loop of humour

Loop of humour

When there's a visible clear loop, in-between the ring/Apollo and the little/Mercury fingers, this is called the loop of humour. Friendly and outgoing, these people enjoy a good laugh and don't take life too seriously. If you have this print, you'll like to go with the flow sharing an optimistic approach, rather than burning the candle at both ends.

Life should be enjoyed and laughter is the best medicine. They always have a great life-work balance, and sometimes turn their passions into thriving and successful businesses, because they know pleasure is a priority.

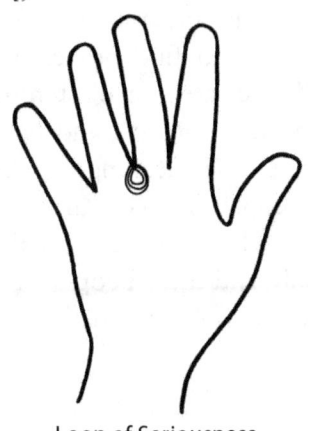

Loop of Seriousness

Loop of seriousness

When there's a clear loop visible in-between the middle/Saturn and ring/Apollo fingers, you are the opposite of the loop of humour, and this is called the loop of seriousness, and is usually found on ambitious, driven people. Duty and responsibility always comes first which gives them the determination and discipline to get ahead or burn out, whichever comes first. It's always

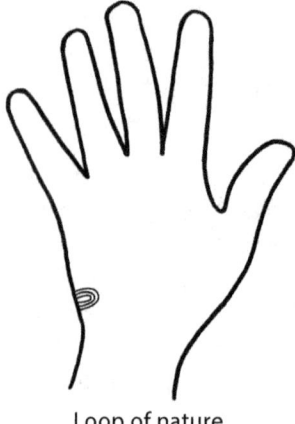
Loop of nature

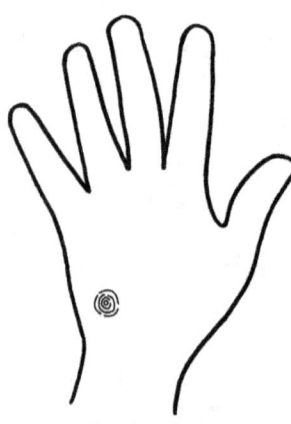
Whorl on Luna

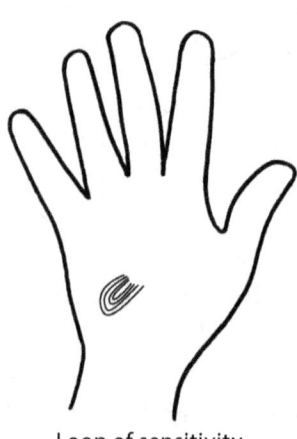
Loop of sensitivity

work before pleasure and to those people around them. They can be seen as rather dull and boring. Mark Twain said, "Never get too busy making a living that you forget to make a life." Every time I see this quote, it reminds me of the person with the loop of seriousness.

Loop of nature

When there's a long loop on the percussion side of Luna, opening towards the lower region, this is somebody who feels the Earth's vibration in its natural architecture. Places like the beach, rivers, rainforests and the countryside, will make you feel at peace, calm and relaxed with not a care in the world, if you have this loop. Deep sleep is always assured after soaking up this beautiful energy. People with the loop of nature, feel at home in these environments.

Whorl on Luna

These people are very sensitive and are so used to being hurt and disrespected by people due to their loving nature. They deliberately like to be and live on their own. Solitude and introspection are ways they like to find peace, and when they talk, they are worth listening to. As they are very spiritual and have great insight into the meanings of the reasons why people face certain challenges in their lives. They are usually gifted artistically, and these people have excellent imaginations and that's why they get great ideas.

Palm prints

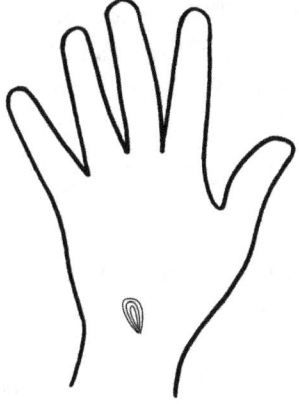
Loop of inspiration

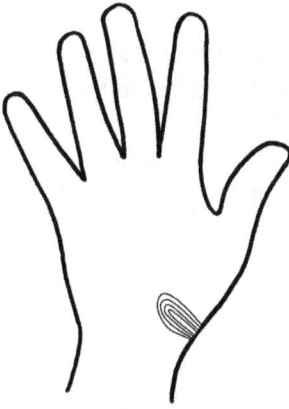
Loop of rhythm

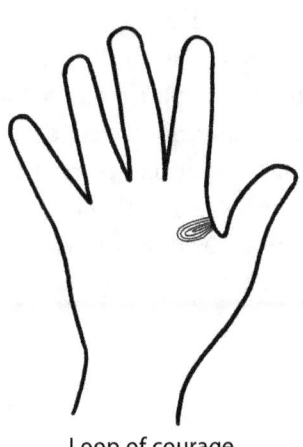
Loop of courage

Loop of sensitivity

If you have a loop pattern on the Mount of Luna, you definitely have strong intuition and are quite sensitive to people and your environment. You have a strong inclination to know when something is not right with people before they even open up their mouths. You definitely can't distort the truth with these people, as they can detect untruths from a mile away. I've also seen this loop on people who enjoy being out on the water, sailing, working on ships at sea, like the Navy, especially when the Mount of Luna is well developed.

Loop of inspiration

This is a very rare loop, but I have seen it on some gifted creative people. It is located in-between the Mounts of Luna and Venus. These talented people get their ideas, insight and inspiration from their intuition, and are always looking out for signs, omens and synchronicity to guide them through life's challenges.

Loop of rhythm

If you have a loop on the Mount of Venus, you'll enjoy music in all its forms. Music is food for your soul so you feel it vibrates right into you. People with this marking enjoy brass instruments such as the saxophone.

Loop of courage

This loop is located pretty close to the inner line of Mars, just on the webbing near the thumb. Just like the Mars line,

141

these people have a lot of energy and passion. They enjoy pushing themselves to the limit. They always go well beyond their call of duty, due to the thrill of achieving challenges they never thought possible. People with this loop are often in the armed forces, or enjoy pursuits like martial arts, where their physical and mental strength is tested.

QUIZ TIME QUESTIONS

1. Will you take life seriously if you have a loop of humour?
2. Does work, duty and responsibility come first with a person who has a loop of seriousness?
3. If you have a whorl on the Mount of Luna, will you have a great imagination?
4. If you've got a loop of courage, would you say your life would be dull and boring?
5. When you have a loop of rhythm, are you gifted musically?
6. People who possess a loop of nature, do they hate being outside in the great outdoors?
7. If you have a loop of sensitivity, could you be a psychic?
8. Is the loop of inspiration a rare palm print?
9. People with a loop of courage, do they enjoy pushing themselves to the limit?
10. Would sailors possess the loop of sensitivity?

Answers:

1. No, these people are optimistic, friendly and like to enjoy life. **2.** Yes, they're serious about their duty to work and life in general. They can be seen as dull and boring. **3.** Yes, these people have great imaginations. **4.** No, these people like to test the limits of who they are. **5.** No, they enjoy music, especially brass instruments in particular. **6.** No, they love nature and are very sensitive to the calming effects that it has on them. **7.** Yes, these people have a strong intuition and are often psychic. **8.** Yes, it is a rare sign. **9.** Always, as they get a thrill out of overcoming challenges that they never thought possible. **10.** Most of the time they do, as well as a thick Mount of Luna.

THIRTEEN

Strange Influencers

If you don't know what you want, others will want you for what they know! You must know yourself. — ISRAELMORE AYIVOR

As you may well have noticed by now, there are small markings which can deplete, enhance, repair, distort or protect the major lines of your hand. When you know what these markings do, they will tell a unique story of what is happening when they appear.

Breaks

 A break is an ending, if it's on the heart line, it can mean a break in a relationship. The head line can be a different way of thinking, from logical reasoning, to using your imagination and creativity with your thought processes. When there is a large gap between the break, you'll feel out of place, and at a loss, but after a short period, you'll start afresh with a different awareness and insight into the reasons that brought on the new change of circumstances, so you won't repeat them in the future. A break is always an ending and a break in lines means change is on the horizon.

Fork

Forks at the end of a line mean two different directions you can take and this creates balance and other opportunities.

Square

When there is a square around a break, this is seen as a positive sign. Squares repair a break, and if you have one, it shows you are taking responsibility for what has happened. In the process you become more evolved, with a depth and understanding to develop the resources to get through and build on the setback that has just occurred to you.

Overlap

 When there is an overlap near a break, which is stronger and clearer than before, this is a positive sign. This is when you have made the best out of a difficult situation, eg on

the life line, there is a break and on the outside of the break an overlap occurs. This means the person has moved on from the break and may have changed relationships, moved to a nicer home in a better location.

Branches (Upward)

When you see small branches running upwards off a major line, there are good times, positive events in your life. These lines empower you and give energy when they appear.

Branches (Downward)

Now if you see the branches run downward off a major line, they can be seen as negative, and disempowering, draining one's energy at this particular time, when they appear.

Chains

A period of time when you found life difficult, perhaps emotionally, mentally or physically.

Frayed line

Can always be found at the beginning or at the end of a line. It is where the line is losing its energy and is depleted.

Double lines

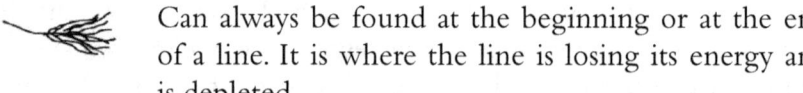

If there are two lines instead of just one, you'll definitely lead quite an interesting and different life. When double lines appear, there's a doubling of energy and enterprise, e.g. a double head line, you may be a lawyer during the day, but think and act differently with your family and friends, or maybe you have two life lines, a home in your native country and another home overseas where you visit frequently. Two fate lines usually mean working two jobs at the same time.

Dots

If you have a dot on the line, the energy becomes intense for you at this particular time. It can be a stressful time in a relationship if seen on the heart line. A new change at work and how you think can be seen with a dot on the head line. Majority of the time it is an intense time, where energy has built up and a situation comes to a head.

Islands

When islands appear on a major line they always indicate stress, confusion or a feeling of going around in circles and not knowing what to do next.

Bar Lines

Little lines that go through a major line always represent interruptions to a person from outside circumstances, eg bar lines going through the life line are usually interruptions or disturbances from family or friends.

Circle

This sign is rare, but indicates a time of confusion and where your freedom is at a standstill.

Grilles

When you see a group of horizontal and vertical lines together forming a grille like pattern, this is a period of stress where your personal energies are scattered. If you see a grille on a mount or around a line, you'll be having difficulty in this particular area. A grille under the ring/Apollo finger means you are having a hard time channelling your creativity, or not having enough fun and happiness in your life.

Star

When you see a star located on a mount or near a line, it indicates shock or a major disruption to a person's life. A star on the mount of Jupiter/Saturn, means you are having a tough time with confidence or self-esteem. The star can be a positive sign when it is found under the Mercury/Apollo mount, and success in the arts or writing, and maybe even fame may be likely.

Triangles

Triangles are usually formed by rising lines and have to be strong and clearly formed to qualify. If formed on your head line, this suggests some type of training or study to advance at work or your career, and is usually seen on doctors, nurses and chiropractors' hands. Whenever triangles are formed on lines or mounts, it does mean you do have a great talent wherever they appear, eg on the

Mount of Luna, great imagination or intuition or under the index/Jupiter finger, high hopes and a large, strong vision of what you want to do in life.

Trident

Y Always found at the end of a line. This sign balances all the properties of the line it is found on. It is usually seen at the end of the heart line and is a positive sign.

Crosses

X ✚ Crosses indicate stress, worry and an unfortunate change, usually something you didn't become aware of until it was too late, and if found under the middle/Saturn finger, you can be a pessimist at times, morbid and even clumsy. When you have a cross under the ring/Apollo finger, you may be having trouble manifesting your creativity into reality due to stagnation. If found under the little/Mercury finger, you have issues with talking the truth, or you lose your business due to poor and unforeseen business deals. But there is a good point here, if you have a cross under the index/Jupiter finger, this is called the happy marriage cross. If you have a cross here, you've got an innate ability to love and nurture your partner at any time in your relationship, good or bad. I've also seen this cross here on a sensitive natural therapists and healers. Please note, don't stress or worry too much as you create your own suffering through your thoughts and actions. People who do this usually suffer from heaviness of the chest due to too much anxiety. By being able to focus in the moment and be more mindful, you too can let go of inner tension and live life with less stress.

QUIZ TIME QUESTIONS

1. What does a break on a line mean?
2. Is a square a positive sign?
3. When there is a break and there is an overlap, is this positive?
4. Upward little vertical lines running off major lines are they positive?
5. If you have two fate lines, what does this mean?
6. What does a dot signify?
7. When an island appears on a line, would you be focussed?

8. Are bar lines running through major lines interruptions from outside influences?
9. Can a star be a positive sign?
10. When triangles are formed on the head line, what does this mean?

Answers:

1. A break in a line indicates an ending of some sort. **2.** Yes, it's positive and signifies protection and using available resources to improve your situation. **3.** Yes, an overlap after a break means you'll come out the other end of the experience in a more favourable light. **4.** Upward little vertical lines are positive and empowering times when they appear. **5.** Most of the time working two jobs at a particular time or on the rare occasion, living different lives with different families. **6.** A dot is an intense time or experience in this person's life when it's seen. **7.** No, islands mean stress and confusion or a setback with an illness. **8.** Yes, they are considered interruptions by challenges people experience by outside influences that most of the time we don't see coming. **9.** Only when found under the Mercury/Apollo mounts which is success in the creative field. **10.** They suggest training or study at the time they appear usually to acquire a job or advance in one's career.

FOURTEEN

Rings

The visual screen in which your destiny is sealed and could be unlocked with intuition and knowledge. — MICHAEL BASSEY JOHNSON

Seeing a ring or rings on your fingers can give you a wealth of insight into the underlying inner conflicts that we all struggle with. Many people subconsciously or subliminally want to improve a particular aspect of their lives, so they put a ring on the finger without realising what is actually taking place, within their lives at a deeper level.

Wearing rings displays that you have challenges going on that need to be sorted out. When the inner conflict has been fixed, the ring will come off this finger and the energy will no longer be stifled. And will be channelled appropriately through the fingertips, creating a proper energy flow, for that particular finger and its characteristics.

Most of the time, you will hear people tell how they love jewellery and adorn themselves with lots of rings. Not so, this person with many rings has a lot going on behind closed doors and have many insecurities. I usually ask, "Why do you wear a ring on this finger?" They usually reply that it's the only finger it will fit on. Not so!

When you look at your rings or a friend's ring, they can tell you a lot about yourself or your friend. For instance, are they plain and simple, or maybe they are loud and obnoxious, saying look at me. Do you have old fashioned values and morals, tried and tested principles, so you might wear antique and stylish rings, or you can have a very elegant and sophisticated ring which gives off the subliminal message that you've got money and power. Everyone, most of the time, are giving off signals to those around them, although the majority aren't aware of it.

What hand are the rings on

Now, if you are wearing rings on the non-dominant hand, but none on the dominant hand, there are some issues that need to be addressed from the past at a deeper level, but you haven't brought them into the now. This energy will deplete your current energy stores.

But if rings are on the same fingers on both hands, you have inner conflicts from the past which you've brought into the present moment.

Now, if there are rings on the dominant hand, but none are on the non-dominant hand, you will be currently having some sort of inner conflict going on in your life. What do we do? We put a ring on the finger which coincides with that particular difficulty of the issue that exists and currently giving you grief.

Rings cut off energy going into the finger tips, which is the life force, the chi or prana (from Eastern philosophy). Rings stifle the energy flow when put on your finger. When you have no rings on any of your fingers, you have a good amount of energy going into yourself, which is great. As you'll be able to direct and focus your energies into the right directions without having any extra emotional and mental concerns to attend to.

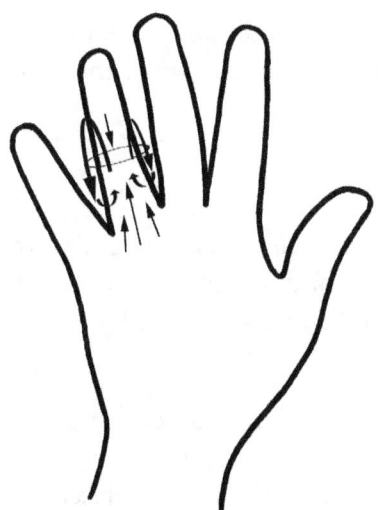

Rings stifle our energy

Having many issues to deal with can be hard on us all, by taking responsibility and the appropriate action and effort, we all can enjoy a happy, fulfilled and meaningful life.

What rings mean when seen on each of the fingers

Index/Jupiter finger

This person is suffering from insecurities about themselves, and are not sure who they are and are wanting to boost their self-esteem and importance. We naturally put a ring on the index/Jupiter finger to get a sense of independence and self-surety.

Middle/Saturn finger

If you want more responsibility, duty and security, you'll put a ring on here. Not only that, if you have a dislike of anyone who is trying to gain authority over you, or trying to give you rules and regulations you don't agree with, on goes the ring on the middle/Saturn finger. This could be someone such as a boss in the workplace, or organisations throwing around their power, police, a boyfriend, wife, husband, girlfriend or the government.

When I give readings to younger females, they usually have a ring on the middle/Saturn finger on the non-dominant hand. This is because they can't let go of past relationships, feelings of hurt or betrayal, or because the relationship with their father was quite negative as he didn't care enough, show affection or wasn't around for her when she was younger before the age of twenty-one.

Most of the time, the person who has this imbalance, will find an older partner to balance this issue and try to reclaim what they lost with their father.

Ring/Apollo finger

Apart from being married and that doesn't count here, if you put a ring on this finger, you are having a difficult time being able to channel your creative energies into the right directions or not having enough fun and enjoyment, feeling bored and discontented.

Little/Mercury finger

When you adorn a ring here, it is a sign of communication problems within relationships, at work, unconventional business dealings or difficulties with sexual matters at the time the ring is placed on the finger.

Thumb

When a ring is placed here, you are being bullied in some way by some one. It can be in a relationship, a group that you belong to that you feel restricted and not free to be yourself. Maybe you want to start something new, but are being held back, for instance a close friend of mine, wore a ring on his dominant hand, meaning after the age of twenty-one and the present moment. He had a wife who had been with him for twenty-three years, so he had a thumb ring for a long period of time. His wife was very domineering and quite the tyrant, telling him what he should and shouldn't do with his work, and life in general. The last time I saw him, the thumb ring was gone and so was his wife. He told me how free he was and was able to breathe for the first time in his life. This is a great example of the reasons why we wear rings.

Rings

When we place a ring on a finger, we have an imbalance in this particular part of our lives. When the issue has been solved, discovered and fixed, the imbalance is no longer in our lives, and off comes the ring.

QUIZ TIME QUESTIONS

1. Are seeing rings on a finger a sign of inner conflicts?
2. By looking at rings on fingers, can they give you an indication of the person's personality and what they are like?
3. Rings worn on the non-dominant hand mean you have issues from the past?
4. If rings are on the same fingers on both hands, you've brought these issues into the present day?
5. If you have some inner conflicts on your dominant hand, but not your non-dominant, that means?
6. Do rings worn on fingers cut off energy going into the finger tips?
7. If you wear a ring on the index/Jupiter finger, are you having an issue with duty and responsibility?
8. If you wear a ring on the middle/Saturn finger, are you having an issue with your self-confidence?
9. Is someone or something taking away your will, if you wear a ring on your thumb?
10. If you adorn a ring on the little/Mercury finger, could you be experiencing sexual difficulties?

Answers:

1. Yes, they're inner issues that the person is dealing with at the particular time they have them on. **2.** Yes, most definitely people who have elegant and sophisticated rings give off the message of money and power. **3.** Yes, before the age of twenty-one. **4.** Issues from the past have been brought into the present day. **5.** You are dealing with imbalances that are not from the past, but are from the present day. **6.** Yes, they cut off the life force of the finger, giving the properties of that particular finger difficulties. **7.** No, there would be insecurities regarding your self-esteem. **8.** No, you would have issues with duty, responsibility or being too serious. **9.** Yes, most definitely could be your partner or family a club you belong to or the workforce. **10.** Yes, sexual difficulties or communication problems.

FIFTEEN

Nails

If you see yourself as other people see you, it means you are lost. You don't know yourself and you have closed down a world class university of diligence. — ISRAELMORE AYIVOR

Nails can tell a lot about us, and how they are kept. Are they manicured, bitten, long, or dirty? These are just small tell-tale signs that we can see that describe a picture when we look at the hands of ourselves and others.

If you look after your nails, you'll also take care of yourself. What you wear throughout the day, everything must match as well as the haircut, even the cleanliness of your home will be in pristine condition. A person who looks after their nails will seriously take pride in themselves and what they want out of life. Career women often have well-kept nails.

How about someone who has dirty nails, or nails that are chipped or broken. Do they have a manual or physical job, or work in a garden as a hobby that they enjoy. That would be fine, but what if they don't. What could this tell you about this person? What would the rest of their lives be like, their appearance, mindset and beliefs? Do you think their home maybe run down or well kept? Things are never black or white, there is always shades of grey, but it is very interesting.

What about ladies who keep their nails long. Do you think they would find it hard to do practical jobs around the house? Would this suggest someone who is impractical?

Do you think people who chew their nails all the way down to the quick, might be anxious and have a tendency to worry, be critical of themselves and others. Look at your nails now, what sort of nails do you have?

By taking a good look at your nails, you can create a great picture of the physical and mental health of ourselves and others. Remember, a picture paints a thousand words.

WHEN YOU SEE

Bitten nails

This person is suffering from stress and anxiety, usually worrying about how other people perceive them. They're impatient with themselves and others, being critical is something they are really good at, especially when they don't get what they want, and they act like a petulant child at times with quite a vicious tongue. These people can hurt others without realising it, not all but most.

Short nails

When the nail is wider than it is long, these people will always follow a set method when living their lives. Analytical and logical, seeing is believing and they can be very opinionated and like to hold their ground even when they've lost an argument. These people can be hard on themselves and rather tactless in speech. They don't suffer fools easily, an can be quite the perfectionists. Afflictions of the heart such as high blood pressure and heart disease are common with short nailed people.

Long nails

When the nail is longer than it is wide, these people are imaginative, creative and intuitive. They enjoy arts, culture and anything pleasing to the eye. They can be very sarcastic, witty and enjoy being sociable but don't like to argue. But when they do watch out, it takes a while for them to get to boiling point, then they just pop like a balloon, letting go of all the stress and tension. If you do have long nails, you may suffer at times with illnesses around the cardiovascular system that is the chest and lungs.

Wedge shaped nails

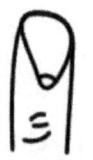

They look like a fan, and are narrow at the bottom and wider at the top. These people are quite sensitive to other people and the environment around them. They tend to take too much on and get depleted very quickly as they worry and stress out too much. I have found people who have wedge shaped nails need to embrace relaxation techniques to quieten their minds which will give them the inner peace they require. Meditation or yoga works wonders for these people.

Oval shaped nails

These people will do anything for you to make you happy. They're always giving and loving, and sometimes when you don't deserve it. They'll focus on others and not enough on themselves. They make good, honest friends, who are loyal, but if you break the bond, they won't. If you double cross them, they will explode into a rage when they have had enough and become stressed when taken advantage of.

Long thin narrow nails

These people can be seen as narcissistic, and only caring about themselves with little regard about anything else. They can be narrow minded and have a hidden agenda to pursue and achieve their goals.

THE THUMB NAIL

Almond shape

These people are sensitive, intuitive and creative and they are a lover of beauty and enjoy the arts.

Square thumb nail

These people are practical and methodical, who always have a set routine to achieve their goals. They've got a lot of determination and perseverance which usually makes them a success.

Oval thumb nail

These people are perfectionists who are very hands on themselves. They always have to do everything the right way, or not at all. Their expectations are very high and most of the time they are very critical of their own abilities. They are good enough, but try to convince them of that.

MEDICAL CONDITIONS WITH THE NAILS

Clubbing of the finger tips

Sometimes the fingertips of the fingers can take on a swollen appearance which gives them a clubbed look.

Clubbed finger tips are always found on heavy smokers and people who have been smoking for a very long time. The swollen appearance of the fingers usually indicates heart or lung disease. At times, healthy young people may have this formation which may be passed down in the family.

Concave nails

If you see a nail that is in a curved formation from the nail bed to its tip. This can be an indication of lung damage. A normal, healthy nail is flat, and usually people with curved nails, so concave, are quite common to have bronchitis, asthma, colds and the flu each winter time. You may also see islands on the life line under the index/Jupiter finger. This person would have suffered from a lung complaint in their childhood.

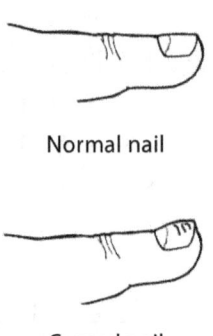

Normal nail

Curved nail

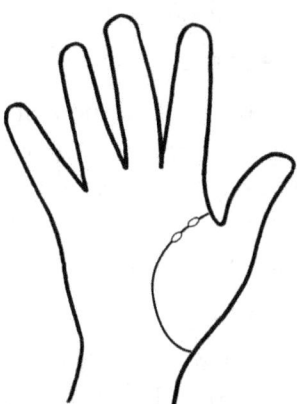

Islands under Jupiter

Watch glass nails

These are also known as a Hippocratic nail. This formation is the exact opposite of the concave nail and is curved outward. People with this nail have problems with the lungs, colds, flus, tuberculosis, tumours on the lung, asthma, as well as heart disease and cirrhosis of the liver. The nail is named after Hippocrates, the father of modern medicine, who identified the nail.

Beau lines

These are the horizontal lines that start at the moon and move towards the tip of the nail. These are from infections and diseases, such as influenza, scarlet fever, measles and pneumonia. You can also have these horizontal ridges appear from a poor diet low in good nutrition as well as a nervous shock to the body's system, such as an emotional stress like the sudden death of a loved one.

Mees' lines

These are horizontal lines on the nail seen after you've experienced fever from a serious illness. Mees' lines have been associated with heart complaints.

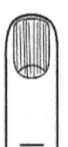

Longitudinal ridges

These ridges stem from someone who has an overactive thyroid gland, skin disorders and rheumatism. If your child has these lines, they may have a fever on its way or rheumatoid arthritis, always check with your doctor.

White spots

If you have white spots or dots on your nails, it's usually because of stress or a mineral deficiency due to poor eating habits. Always eat a healthy diet and check with a certified nutritionist, to check if you are eating the right foods for your blood type and body.

Moons

When there are half-moons visible on the nails, the blood circulation and health are in a good condition.

Always make sure the cuticles have been pushed back to reveal a half-moon, as the visibility of moons can come down to taking care of your nails.

Pale or non-existent moons

If the moons are pale or non-existent, the blood circulation and immune system will be down. This is usually caused by stress, feeling uptight, taking life too seriously, without any enjoyment or down time. Usually, I have found as well, that the hands and feet are cold due to the poor blood circulation. If the moons have a blue tinge to them, then there can be a problem with the heart and lungs, and a stroke could be possible. Large moons can indicate an overactive thyroid.

WHAT COLOUR ARE YOUR NAILS?

Red nails

These indicate stress and tension with high blood pressure and a hostile temperament.

Pink nails

These indicate good blood circulation.

Blue nails

These indicate poor blood circulation and an imbalance with the heart and lungs.

White nails

This indicates no energy or vitality and liver or kidney problems, chronic smoking affecting the nervous system, as well as an iron deficiency.

Spots and blemishes

These are an indication of a deficiency in vitamins and minerals. People with spots on the nails worry too much, as they are a sign of nervous tension.

QUIZ TIME QUESTIONS — NAILS

1. When you see bitten nails, would they be relaxed and a calm type of person?
2. Do short nailed people use their intuition and imagination a lot?
3. Would you say, long nailed people are practical and logical?
4. People who have wedge shaped nails, would they be loud and obnoxious?
5. Do oval shaped nails care about themselves a lot, and be seen as narcissistic?
6. People with long thin narrow nails, would they be caring and worried about other people's needs before their own?
7. Would you say the almond shaped thumb nailed person is intuitive and creative?
8. Would a person with a square thumb nail, have a set way of doing things?

9. Would you say the oval shaped thumb nailed person be self-critical and have high expectations?
10. Would someone with long nails be seen as impractical?

Answers:

1. No, this person is suffering from stress and anxiety. They can be quite the worriers. **2.** No, these people are very logical, seeing is believing for these people. **3.** No, these people are very intuitive, creative and imaginative. **4.** No, these people are very sensitive and introverted, who like to enjoy their own company or people who are similar to them. **5.** No, these people are giving and loving, caring for others is what they like to do. **6.** No, they can be seen as narcissistic and narrow minded. **7.** Yes, they're creative and intuitive who enjoy beauty in all its forms. **8.** Yes, they always have a set method and have a lot of determination to achieve their wishes. **9.** Yes, they're perfectionists who can be very hard on themselves at times. **10.** Yes, they could be seen as impractical, as with long nails. They might not be able to do work around the house, in the garden or workplace arenas.

QUIZ TIME QUESTIONS — NAILS — MEDICAL CONDITIONS

1. If you have swollen finger tips, could you be a smoker?
2. What does club finger tips indicate?
3. If someone has a concave nail, what does this indicate?
4. When an island appears under the index/Jupiter finger on the life line, what does this indicate?
5. When a nail is curved outward, the opposite of a concave nail, what is this type of nail called?
6. When there are horizontal lines on a nail, what is this called?
7. When there's longitude lines on a nail, what does this indicate?
8. If there are half-moons on a nail, is this a good sign of good blood circulation?
9. If you have a blue colour to your nail, does this indicate poor blood circulation?
10. If you have spots and blemishes on your nails, would you be eating the right diet to get the correct amount of vitamins and minerals?

Answers:

1. Yes, most definitely, long term smokers. **2.** It indicates heart or lung disease. **3.** It indicates people who suffer from asthma, bronchitis and the flu causing lung damage. **4.** This island indicates a lung complaint when a child or adolescent. **5.** This nail is called the Hippocratic nail, named after Hippocrates, the father of modern medicine. **6.** Horizontal lines on a nail is called Beau lines. **7.** Longitude lines on a nail indicate an overactive thyroid gland. These people can suffer from skin disorders, and rheumatoid arthritis. **8.** Yes. **9.** Yes, poor blood circulation and an imbalance with the heart and lungs. **10.** No, spots and blemishes appear on nails when there's deficiencies of vitamins and minerals within a person's diet, it can also be a sign of nervous tension.

SIXTEEN

Guidelines to Give a Great Reading

Just as a pebble thrown into the water creates ripples, so our thoughts create similar effects on our palms. — MICHAEL SCOTTS

If you enjoy palmistry as much as I do, and you'd like to read for family, friends and others, I have written out these guidelines for you to live by. To give the best and most appropriate reading you can perform.

Rule One: Be open and friendly, build a good rapport, always make sure your mind is quiet and you have a positive space to work in.

Rule Two: Ask the age of your client, so you know where they are on the major lines of the hand, (e.g. life line, fate line, head line).

Rule Three: Express yourself in a clear concise manner, with open body language. Limit questions to only what's relevant to the reading.

Rule Four: Work systematically through the hand, so you cover all aspects of the client's life.

Rule Five: Be tactful, and choose your words carefully. Don't act surprised at what you see. As your client will be hanging on your every word, you need to show respect and place importance on the other person's feelings.

Rule Six: Don't ever prophesize death or serious illness, because you can't. Make sure you leave your ego at the door, and don't let the thank-yous go to your head.

Rule Seven: Prepare to make mistakes and don't act like you know it all. At times your friends and clients will disagree with you. These moments are great for your professional development, to become a better palmist. You must listen and learn how to handle each situation in the appropriate manner.

Rule Eight: Sometimes people will lie to you, because they're not ready to accept or admit certain information. Respect that and move on, never judge or play holier than thou.

Rule Nine: Proceed slowly and investigate all information, before you express yourself. Balance your observations with both the passive and active hands. There are always contradictory and complementary aspects, always create a positive picture and a pleasant experience, for the both of you.

Rule Ten: Look for the unique aspects of the lines and prints. Everyone has something special that defines who they are. Let go of anything average and focus on what illuminates the very essence of the person in front of you.

Rule Eleven: Always be ethical in your readings, and maintain the confidentiality of your friends and clients.

SEVENTEEN

When you want to read for others

A reminder, always be:
- Open and friendly.
- Positive and supportive.
- Be congruent with what you say with your body language.
- Selective with the questions you ask, so they are relevant to the reading.
- Respectful, and place importance on your client's feelings and culture.
- Helpful and understanding.
- Down to earth, and leave your ego at the door.
- Prepared to make mistakes.
- Non-judgemental and accepting by the untruths to what people may say to cover up what they don't want to accept.
- On the look-out for anything that stands out and let go of anything average. It is in your uniqueness that makes everyone special.
- Reading both hands, so you get the complete picture, as there are many contradictory and complementary aspects when reading.
- Creative and use your imagination to give your client a memorable and uplifting experience.
- Never prophesise illness or death.
- Be patient with yourself and others.
- Love in action, which is love in service, working for the greater good for all of human kind is your main objective.

EIGHTEEN

Last Words

Whoever has self-knowledge, the world cannot contain them —*JESUS*

Congratulations on making it to the end of the book, I commend you on your dedication and perseverance. I hope you've found Know Thyself an interesting and insightful read. As this was my full intention to open up your minds and those of your children, to know the true nature of who you truly are.

My role to bring light and knowledge to you and your loved ones was of the utmost importance to me. When you know thyself and that of the people who are important to you. You can encourage them to strengthen their talents and abilities and iron out any limitations you place upon yourself and be the best that you can be. By becoming accountable and knowing your true self, you become an amazing gift to yourself and those you meet every day.

Please pass this book on and may the true wisdom within its pages enlighten and inspire you to Know Thyself and live the life that you've imagined.

Much love always
Luke Edward Sheedy.

NINETEEN
Further Reading

Here is a list of books I have enjoyed on the insightful art of palmistry.

- Peter Hazel, *New Age Palmistry*, 1989, Lothian Publishing, Melbourne.
- Johnny Fincham, *Palmistry – From Apprentice To Pro In Twenty-four Hours*, 2007, O Books, United Kingdom.
- Cheiro, *Palmistry For All*, 2008, Nabu press, Charleston, South Carolina.
- Andrew Fitzherbert, *Hand Psychology*, 1986, Angus & Robertson, Sydney.

"All you need in life is to know thyself; to live with the knowledge that it's just life, and that's the way it is. You need a sense of what your life means to you, the appreciation of yourself, your friendships and the love of others. You need a desire to grow as a person to discover what your gifts in life are to yourself, others and the world. Embrace who you are…" —— James A. Murphy

Other works by the author

Discover Your Path, Your Life is Worth Living

If you feel you've lost direction in life, have strayed from your path in your career or relationship, or not living a happy or fulfilled life, then *Discover Your Path, Your Life is Worth Living* is the book for you.

In this book, Luke Sheedy provides the tools, exercises and strategies to guide you, to push you, and give you encouragement and the confidence to bring purpose, meaning and freedom back into your life.

Discover your true potential and start living your dreams awake. This is a manual for living the life you want. Take this epic journey of self-discovery where your new life awaits you. The time is now – your life is in your hands.

www.lukesheedy.com

www.ingramcontent.com/pod-product-compliance
Lightning Source LLC
Chambersburg PA
CBHW050552300426
44112CB00013B/1884